Horizons

Geography 11–14

David Gardner
Roger Knill
John Smith

Nelson Thornes
a Wolters Kluwer business

Published in 2006 by:
Nelson Thornes Ltd
Delta Place
27 Bath Road
CHELTENHAM
GL53 7TH
United Kingdom

06 07 08 09 10 / 10 9 8 7 6 5 4 3 2 1

A catalogue record for this book is available from the British Library

ISBN 0 7487 9051 9

Edited by Katherine James
Picture research by Liz Savery
Illustrations by Gordon Lawson, Angela Lumley, Richard Morris, David Russell Illustration
Page make-up by eMC Design, www.emcdesign.org.uk

Printed in Croatia by Zrinski

Acknowledgements

With thanks to the following for permission to reproduce photographs and other copyright material in this book:

Cover photo: Corel 610 (NT)

Alamy/ Bill Bachmann: p.80A; Alamy/ bobo: p.59A (top); Alamy/ G P Bowater: p.19C; Alamy/ Sue Cunningham Photographic: p.112D; Alamy/ Keith Dannemiller: p.44D; Alamy/ Beth Dixson: p58B (top right); Alamy/ David R Frazier Photolibrary, Inc: p.84C; Alamy/ Chloe Hall: p.40A; Alamy/ Andrew Holt: p.59A (bottom); Alamy/ LifeFile Photos Ltd pp.89, 90; Alamy/ Iain Masterton: p.41G; Alamy/ Network Photographers: p.94C; Alamy/ Pacific Press Service: p.10A; Alamy/ Edward Parker: p.115B; Alamy/ Robert Harding Picture Library Ltd: p.12C; Alamy/ The Photolibrary Wales: p.45F; Alamy/ Transtock Inc: p.56A (left); Alamy/ WR Publishing: p58B (bottom left); BrazilPhotos/ Ricardo Funari: p.109E; Corbis/ Yann Arthus-Bertrand: p.108B; Corbis/ Gary Braasch: p.41F; Corbis/ Douglas Engle: p.118A; Corbis/ Macduff Everton: p.33D; Corbis/ Paulo Fridman: p.122A (bottom left); Corbis/ Fukuhara, Inc: p.58B (top left); Corbis/James Robert Fuller: p.20A; Corbis/ Joao Luiz Bulcao: p.122A (top right); Corbis/ Layne Kennedy: p.122A (bottom right); Corbis/ Owaki-Kulla: p.47B; Corbis/ Douglas Peebles: p.12B; Corbis/ Reuters: p.60B; Corbis/ Reuters/ Denis Balibouse: p.119B; Corbis/ Reuters/ Pierre Holtz: p.42D; Corbis/ Alan Schein Photography: p.58A (background); Corbis/ Tom Van Sant: Front Cover Resource A; Corel 12 (NT): p.44C; Corel 29 (NT): p.105G; Corel 40 (NT): p.104C; Corel 118 (NT): p.44B; Corel 561 (NT): p.70B (left); Digital Vision 1 (NT): p.40B; Digital Vision 15 (NT): p.111G; Gerry Ellis/ Digital Vision JA (NT): p.104B, 105F; Gerry Ellis/ Michael Durham/ Digital Vision LC (NT): p.105E; eStock Photo/ Alamy p.58B (whole); FAMOUS Pictures & Features Agency: p.56A (bottom); David and Brenda Floyd: pp.72/73A, 73B, 75G, 76B, 78C, 80/81C, 81 (top right and bottom left); FLPA/ Minden Pictures/ Michael & Patricia Fogden: p.105H; FLPA/ Minden Pictures/ Frans Lanting: p.108D; FLPA/ Minden Pictures/ Mark Moffett: p.104/105A (whole); Stephen Frink/ Digital Vision LL (NT): p.66A; David Gardner: pp.36A, F, 125; Getty: p.108/109A; Getty/ AFP: p.4B; Getty Images/ National Geographic: p.111E; Getty/ The Image Bank: p.56A (top right); Getty Images/ Time Life Pictures: pp. 112/113A, 112B, 113C; Lizzie Houghton: p.65C; Insight-Visual/ Steve Forrest: p.17B; Magnum Photos: p.60A; Suzanne Mehmet: p.36B and C; MODIS images courtesy of NASA's Terra satellite, supplied by Ted Scambos, National Snow and Ice Data Center, University of Colorado: p.87B; NASA satellite images (developed by The Earth Observatory Team): pp.55B and C,106A; NASA satellite image from http://visibleearth.nasa.gov, Jacques Descloitres, MODIS Land Rapid Response Team, NASA/GSFC: Back Cover Resource D; naturepl.com/ Peter Oxford: p.104D; John Norbury: pp.64A, 70B (right); Nordicphotos/ Alamy: p.16A; Panos/ Martin Adler: p.8A; Panos/ Tim Hetherington: p.32B; Panos/ Rob Huibers: p.14A; Panos/ Gerd Ludwig: p.122A (top left); Panos/ Caroline Penn: p.32C, 95E; Panos/ Sean Sprague:p.114A; Pictorial Press/ Alamy: p.58A (left); Omari Pofu: p.36D; Practical Action/Annie Bungeroth: p.40D; Rex/ Action Press: p.21C; Rex/ Bruce Bailey: p.109C; Rex/ Keiran Dodds: p.59A (middle); Rex/ DigitalGlobe: p.4A ; Rex/ Patrick Frilet: p.82C; Rex/ Paul Grover: p.42B; Rex/ Richard Gardner: p.93D; Rex/ Jacques Jangoux: p.111D; Rex/ Sipa Press: pp.5D, 11B, 12A, 32A, 41H; Gilles Saussier: p.101E; Science Photo Library/ Dr Morley Read: p.68/69B; Science Photo Library/ M-Sat Ltd: pp.116B and C; John Smith: pp.64B, 82B, 84/85A, 90B, 92A, 96A, 99D, 100B, 101D, 124 (both); Still Pictures/ Edgar Cleijne: p.24/25C; Still Pictures/ Mark Edwards: pp.40C, 41E; Still Pictures/ Peter Frischmuth: p.83F; Still Pictures/ Ron Giling: p.44A; Still Pictures/ Hartmut Schwarzbach: p.24A; Still Pictures/ Friedrich Stark: p.100A; Still Pictures/ Charlotte Thege: p.33E; Still Pictures/ Manfred Vollmer: p.103C; Still Pictures/ UNEP/ S Belon Lopez: p.101F; Still Pictures/ UNEP/ J Vallespir: p.13D; Still Pictures/ WWI/ Adrian Dorst: p.85D; Still Pictures/ WWI/ Mark Hamblin: pp.85F and G; Still Pictures/ WWI/ Jorgen Schytte: p.91; Still Pictures/ WWI/ David Woodfall: p.64/65D; Stone/ Donald Nausbaum: p.110B; Sunset Avenue Productions/ Digital Vision WA (NT): p.44/45E; Benjamin Wachenje: p.35C; Frederick Wilson: p.92B; Woodfall Wild Images pp.83E and 85E.

With thanks to CAFOD, CARE International and Médecins Sans Frontières UK for permission to reproduce their logos (21D).

Logo reproduced from Save the Children (21D).

The Oxfam logo (21D) is reproduced with the permission of Oxfam GB, Oxfam House, John Smith Drive, Cowley, Oxford OX4 2JY, UK www.oxfam.org.uk. Oxfam GB does not necessarily endorse any text or activities that accompany the materials.

Development compass rose (25B) and proportional maps (28A and B) reproduced with kind permission of TIDE (Teachers in Development Education) from the 'What is Development?' pack.

Screenshot (30C) reproduced with permission of World Bank.

Screenshot (34B) reproduced from www.makepovertyhistory.org.

'Three Rs will help to light up Kenyan pupils', courtesy of the Scarborough Evening News, 18 June 2005 (37E).

With thanks to the Fairtrade Foundation for permission to reproduce two spreads from their information pamphlet (39B).

'Ay caramba! Mexican Food on Target to Outsell Chinese' by Louise Barnett, Independent Online, 4 June 2005, and reproduced with permission (59E).

'Game 'Carnage' in Tanzania Alarms Kenya', 4 February 2002, reproduced from The East African (80B).

With thanks to the Cumbria Fells and Dales LEADER+ programme for permission to reproduce their logo (92B).

With thanks to Christian Aid for granting permission to adapt their water calculator artwork (102A).

Screenshot (117D) reproduced from www.ran.org.

Screenshot (117E) reproduced from www.brazilbrazil.com.

Screenshot (120A) reproduced with permission of Southern Cross Tours & Expeditions.

'Brazil Creates Largest Rainforest Reserve', 23 August 2002, reproduced from BBC News at bbcnews.com (p.121).

With thanks to Raintree Nutrition, Inc. for permission to reproduce their logo and a photograph of their products (121C).

Every effort has been made to contact copyright holders and we apologise if any have been overlooked.

contents

1 Tectonics

Is your world moving you?

Where are we going?

In this unit you will learn:

- **how the internal structure of the Earth affects people living on the surface**

- **to understand how plate movements cause earthquakes and volcanoes**

- **how people live with the threat of earthquakes and volcanoes**

- **to develop an awareness of how places are interdependent through aid.**

Before

After

Banda Aceh, Indonesia, 2004. The tsunami changed some aspects of the region's geography for ever. What are the human and physical impacts in the disaster zone? **A**

Country	Confirmed dead
Indonesia	173 981
Sri Lanka	38 195
India	10 744
Thailand	5322
Somalia	298
Myanmar	90
Malaysia	68–74
Maldives	82
Seychelles	1–3
Tanzania	10
Bangladesh	2
South Africa	2
Kenya	1
Yemen	1
Total (approx.)	**228 800**

C How could this happen in the 21st century? The death toll from the Indonesian earthquake, 2004

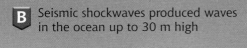

B Seismic shockwaves produced waves in the ocean up to 30 m high

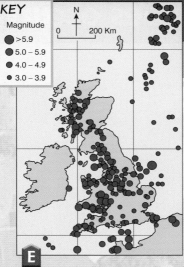

KEY

Magnitude
- ● >5.9
- ● 5.0 – 5.9
- ● 4.0 – 4.9
- ● 3.0 – 3.9

N

0   200 Km

E

Movers and shakers: is the Earth moving in your town? This map shows recorded earthquakes affecting the British Isles. On average, small earthquakes occur here every four days.

You are unlikely to be more than 150 km away from a volcano in Britain but it will probably be over 50 million years old and extinct. Figure **E** shows that we are closer to an earthquake than we think. How we are affected by earth movements depends on time and place.

The planet you are standing on is 4 600 000 000 years old. It has changed every day of those 4.6 billion years and will be different again tomorrow. Many of the changes are taking place at such a slow speed that we cannot see them happen. (The UK is moving away from the USA at about 2 cm/year.) They are predictable events. Other changes happen so quickly that we cannot escape them (for example, a volcanic ash flow can move downhill at over 100 km/h). These more unpredictable events may threaten life and are called **natural hazards**. The energy which drives all the events that shape our physical world lies deep within the Earth. The study of how that energy creates, distorts and destroys the thin crust we live on is called **plate tectonics**. It affects everyone, even people in the UK.

D

Devastating power, or photo opportunity? 10% of the world's population live under threat from the 500+ active **volcanoes**.

Key Words!

Natural hazards

Events which cause damage or destruction to our natural environment, our built environment and our way of life, e.g. earthquakes, volcanoes, floods, hurricanes and tsunamis.

Plate tectonics

The idea that the Earth's surface is divided into a number of plates which move slowly across the globe.

OVER TO YOU

1. What is a 'natural hazard'?

2. Explain how earthquakes and volcanoes can be described as natural hazards.

3. Working with a partner, write down the three most important factors that you think determine whether people living in different parts of the world are at risk from earthquakes and/or volcanoes or not. (We will come back to these three factors at the end of this unit.)

Comune
di NICOLOSI
m 1900 s.l.m.

Where do earthquakes and volcanoes occur?

Our Earth has been changing and cooling down since it was formed, and this is still happening. The planet creates its own heat by radioactive decay of elements and by the generation of heat as some heavier elements sink towards the centre. This heat is trapped by the colder crust, which is not one piece but many plates in constant motion (map *E*). Convection currents are created by the heat and they drag the plates apart in some areas and push them together in others.

- In some places the crust is created (**constructive margins**).
- In other areas it is destroyed (**destructive margins**).
- At **collision zones** it is buckled by pressure into mountain ranges.
- At **slip margins** plates slide past one another.

Many areas of the world are far away from these active plate margins and may seem safe. But even in the UK, which is in the middle of a plate, we are still pushed around by the conveyor belt of crust that is constantly being made and destroyed elsewhere.

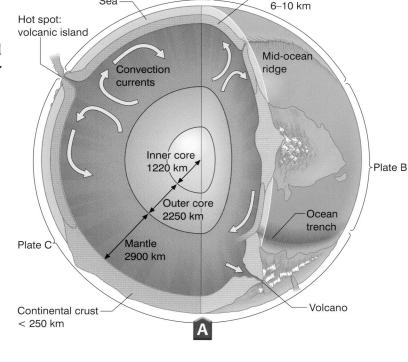

A

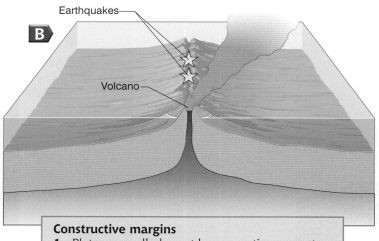

B

Constructive margins
1. Plates are pulled apart by convection currents.
2. Basalt lava seeps in to form new crust beneath the sea.
3. Much of the magma is intruded as dolerite dykes (thin sheets of igneous rock).
4. New lava and dykes add extra crust at each side of the spreading ridge.

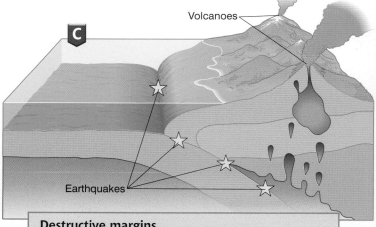

C

Destructive margins
1. Where plates collide, the denser plate slides beneath the lighter one (**subduction**).
2. The descending plate creates friction and a build-up of pressure which causes partial melting of the crust, and earthquakes.
3. Magma (molten rock) from below the crust can rise to form volcanoes.

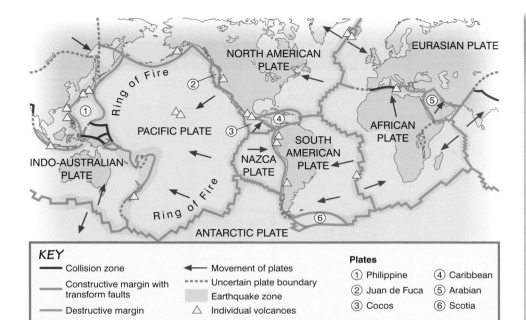

KEY

		Plates	
■ Collision zone	← Movement of plates	① Philippine	④ Caribbean
Constructive margin with transform faults	···· Uncertain plate boundary	② Juan de Fuca	⑤ Arabian
Destructive margin	▨ Earthquake zone	③ Cocos	⑥ Scotia
	△ Individual volcanoes		

E

Key Words!

Constructive margin
Where plates pull apart from each other and new crust is made.

Destructive margin
Where plates crash into each other and crust is destroyed.

Slip (or passive) margin
Where plates slide past each other and crust is neither made nor destroyed.

Subduction zone
Where plates made of ocean crust slide beneath other plates they have collided with and are eventually consumed.

Convection currents
Movements in the semi-molten rocks of the upper mantle caused by rising heat. They move the plates around.

Earth structure
The Earth is made of three main layers.

- The **crust** is between 6 and 70 km thick. It is divided into oceanic crust and continental crust.
  - Continental crust is the least dense, most varied and thickest type on average (20–70 km). It is made of granitic materials.
  - Oceanic crust is very uniform (6–11 km). It is made almost entirely of basaltic lava and dykes.
- The **mantle** is made of denser rocks than the crust and makes up about 80% of the Earth's volume. It is hot, and although it is solid it behaves like a thick liquid and can move over time.
- The **core** is rich in iron and nickel. The outer core is liquid and the inner core is solid.

D

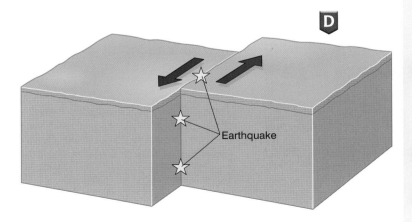

Earthquake

Slip margins
1. Where plates rub past each other, friction builds up and energy is released when the plates 'jerk', causing earthquakes.
2. Little heat is generated, so volcanoes are rare in these locations.

OVER TO YOU

1 Make a simple copy of diagram **A** and add the following labels:
- Thickest crust
- Thickest layer
- Most iron-rich zone
- Most liquid zone
- Coolest zone
- Densest zone.

2 Use map **E** to help you *describe* the distribution of earthquakes and volcanoes.

Hint: Think about how close to, or far from, the plate margins they are.

3 *Explain* the worldwide distribution of earthquakes and volcanoes.

4 Using the following terms, explain how crust can be made and destroyed.

- destructive margin ● basalt ● volcano
- subduction ● spreading ridge
- constructive margin ● melting ● dykes
- convection currents ● earthquake

What happens in an earthquake?

The Indonesian earthquake of 26 December 2004 was the fourth biggest earthquake since 1900 – it measured 9.0 on the Richter scale. Like many such events it only lasted for a few seconds – but the devastation caused by the *tsunami* that followed was greater than any recorded tectonic event in recent history. Tsunamis are relatively unusual, especially ones this size. However, earthquakes are more common than we think.

Any large movement in the Earth can lead to an earthquake. Some of our worst earthquakes happen when plates collide or rub past each other at plate margins. Friction prevents the plates from moving past each other easily. Pressure builds up in the crust. This may be relieved by a sudden earth movement and the release of energy is what we experience as an earthquake. But just like releasing one end of a spring, it may take a while for the ground to settle down afterwards, so aftershocks are often experienced for some time after a big 'quake. The Indonesian earthquake was rapidly followed by further earthquakes in the region, in February 2005 (measuring 6.7) and March 2005 (8.7).

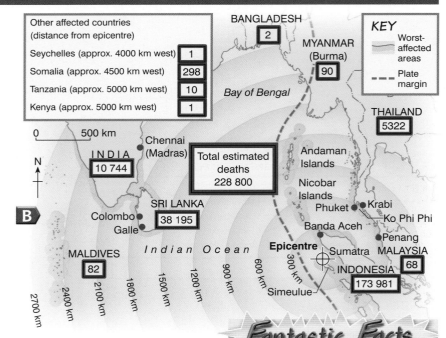

B

Other affected countries (distance from epicentre)	
Seychelles (approx. 4000 km west)	1
Somalia (approx. 4500 km west)	298
Tanzania (approx. 5000 km west)	10
Kenya (approx. 5000 km west)	1

KEY
— Worst-affected areas
--- Plate margin

BANGLADESH 2
MYANMAR (Burma) 90
Bay of Bengal
THAILAND 5322
Chennai (Madras)
INDIA 10 744
Total estimated deaths 228 800
Andaman Islands
Nicobar Islands
Phuket — Krabi
— Ko Phi Phi
SRI LANKA 38 195
Colombo
Galle
Banda Aceh
Penang
Indian Ocean
Epicentre Sumatra MALAYSIA 68
MALDIVES 82
INDONESIA 173 981
Simeulue

Fantastic Facts

- The death toll from the Indonesian earthquake and tsunami was put at more than 228 800 (it included 124 UK citizens, with 21 missing, feared dead).
- The largest recorded earthquake in the world – in Chile on 22 May 1960 – had a magnitude of 9.5.

As the Indian Plate subducted beneath the Burma micro-plate, tensions built up, over centuries. These were released suddenly in 2004 as a fault line shifted a distance of 20 metres.

A

C

(5) Seismic energy is transferred to the water and tsunami waves develop.

(4) Sudden movement along fault lines causes a huge submarine landslide.

Sea level

Indian Ocean

(3) Rocks buckle and fold, and pressure builds up.

Indo-Australian plate

Eurasian plate

(1) The Indo-Australian plate is pushed towards and subducts beneath the Eurasian plate.

(2) Friction leads to build-up of stress.

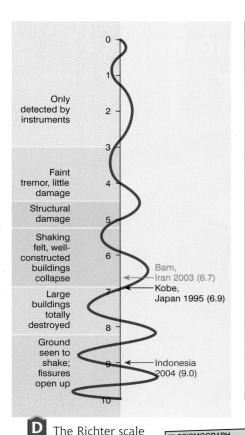

D The Richter scale

Only detected by instruments

Faint tremor, little damage

Structural damage

Shaking felt, well-constructed buildings collapse

Large buildings totally destroyed

Ground seen to shake; fissures open up

Bam, Iran 2003 (6.7)
Kobe, Japan 1995 (6.9)
Indonesia 2004 (9.0)

Key Words!

Tsunami

A giant wave or series of large waves in the ocean created by major shallow-water earthquakes and/or submarine landslides.

Liquefaction

The process in an earthquake when the movement of energy waves causes the ground to act like a liquid.

Magnitude

A measure of how much energy is released by an earthquake.

Intensity

A measure of the effect of an earthquake.

Seismic shockwaves (diagram **E**) shake the ground, causing rigid buildings to collapse. A large 'quake may shake the earth so much that it fails to act like a solid any more and **liquefaction** occurs as the ground moves like water. Such movements can be devastating for any buildings or gas or water pipes in the area.

The amount of energy released by an earthquake is called its **magnitude**. This is the measure on the Richter scale (diagram **D**) from 1 to 10. Every step on the scale is 30 times greater than the one before. So a scale of 5, for example, is a lot less worrying than a scale of 9 (as experienced in Indonesia).

The **intensity** of an earthquake is a measure of how it affects the land, so it is measured in terms of the damage caused. The effects will be far worse in areas where the ground is soft or where buildings are less well-constructed.

A seismometer drew **E** this record of an earthquake, which is called a seismograph

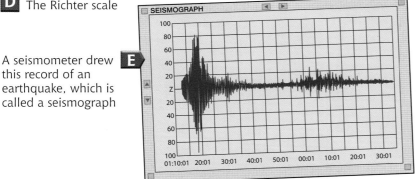

SEISMOGRAPH

Seismic waves stronger along fault line
Shockwaves
Epicentre
Energy decreases away from the epicentre
F
Focus

OVER TO YOU

1 State whether each of these is *true* or *false*, and try to explain why.
  a **Magnitude** is a measure of the energy released by an earthquake.
  b Earthquake magnitude and **intensity** are measures of the same thing.
  c Places close to the **epicentre** experience a stronger effect than places further away.
  d A **seismometer** measures the shaking of the ground.

  e The **Richter scale** is an earthquake measuring machine.
  f Old or weaker **buildings** are very safe in an earthquake.
  g Most earthquakes last for less than **10 seconds**.
  h **Aftershocks** rarely follow after an earthquake.

2 Draw a simple concept map to explain the links between the terms shown in **bold text** in question 1. Add extra links using ideas from these two pages, e.g. *seismic, tsunami, focus.*

3 Earthquake warning systems are very expensive. Write a paragraph to explain why it might be a good idea for wealthier countries to help all countries to have a seismic warning system.

Hint: Think about:
● the issue in terms of humanitarian, scientific and economic factors
● how many countries were affected by a single earthquake in the Indonesian tsunami.

WEBLINKS **You will find a link giving more information about earthquakes in the UK and around the world at** www.nelsonthornes.com/horizons

Do all earthquakes have the same impact?

Where we live has a big influence on how likely we are to experience an earthquake. How we are affected by such events may have a lot more to do with the country we live in.

A

Why can't wealthy nations defend themselves against earthquakes?

B What could have stopped these buildings collapsing on their inhabitants?

OVER TO YOU

Our ability to predict when and where events will happen and how prepared we are to prevent the worst effects, often depends upon the country's wealth and the level of development. Japan and Iran are both in regions that frequently experience earthquakes. How they prepare for, are affected by, and deal with major earthquakes can tell us a lot about the global differences in how countries respond to tectonic events.

C Fact file for Kobe in Japan, and Bam in Iran

Location	Kobe, Japan	Bam, Iran
Magnitude	6.9	6.6
Deaths	5 200	31 000
Injured	36 896	30 000
Damage	$150 billion	$32.7 million
Homeless	310 000	75 600
Country's wealth (GNP/person)	$40 100	$7 700
Population	1 513 967	78 400

WEBLINKS

You will find a link giving more information about earthquakes in Japan and Iran at www.nelsonthornes.com/horizons

Advanced organiser

You are going to write a report comparing the effects of a similar event in two very different countries: Japan (Kobe 1995) and Iran (Bam 2003). In comparing these two events you are aiming to test this hypothesis: 'The impact of earthquakes depends on the wealth of the country affected.'

- Fact file **C** and other information on these pages is only the start. You will need to use the weblinks provided on the Horizons website.
- **Smart search** The web is full of information you need, and even more that you don't! To search effectively, even on sites you know are relevant, you need to be clear what it is you are looking for.
- **Categories** You will need information on similar aspects of the earthquakes for both countries, so think about what those are. They might include location maps, casualty figures, damage to buildings, roads and communications, business and trade, estimated costs. To compare effectively you will need information from each country on these key issues.
- *Remember:* 'Comparing' doesn't mean just listing what happened in two different places. It means explaining the similarities *and* the differences.
- **Conclusion** You must decide if the hypothesis is true or not, based on the evidence you have collected. Whether you agree or disagree, you need to explain your decision, weighing up the evidence and raising any other ideas or aspects that you think are important.

Volcanoes – hazards, or holiday destinations?

Volcanoes are some of the most dramatic natural hazards on the planet. Photos *A* and *B* show just how dangerous they can be when lava erupts at over 800°C, ash smothers the landscape or volcanic bombs rain down. Yet many people live next to volcanoes and many profit from them (photo *D*). Iceland uses low-cost power from geothermal energy, and the fertile volcanic soils on the slopes of Vesuvius in Italy support some of the best farming in the area. To decide if volcanoes are friend or foe we need to look at them more closely.

A

B

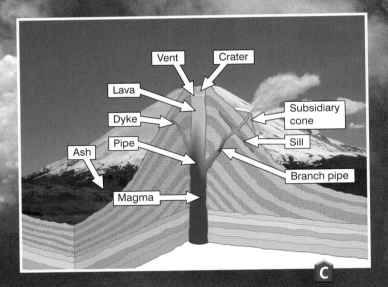

Vent

Crater

Lava

Dyke

Subsidiary cone

Pipe

Sill

Ash

Branch pipe

Magma

C

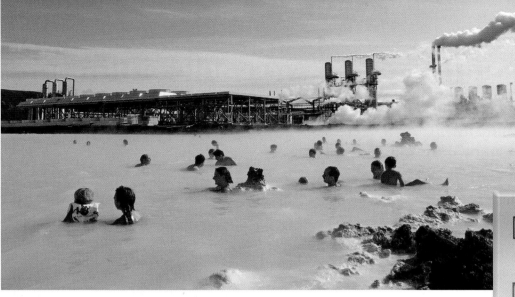

D A tourist snap shows how dramatic volcanic scenery and geothermal power attract many visitors

Volcanoes are formed when **magma** escapes to the surface through an opening or vent. When the magma reaches the surface it is called **lava** and becomes more mobile, as there is less pressure at the surface. If the vent is blocked by cold, solid lava, pressure builds up and the following eruption can be explosive. Ash and volcanic bombs may be blown from the crater over a wide area. The lava that pours out often follows predictable routes, so people can live close by quite safely. However, predicting how dangerous an eruption will be may require life or death decisions.

Fantastic Facts

- Around 20–30 volcanoes erupt each year.
- There are around 500 active volcanoes around the world.
- Iceland uses volcanic heat to grow more bananas than any other European country.

Key Words!

Active volcano

One that has erupted within living memory.

Dormant volcano

A volcano that is 'asleep' – it has erupted within recorded history.

Extinct volcano

One that will never erupt again.

Lava

Molten rock that has reached the surface of the Earth.

Magma

Molten rock still within the Earth.

OVER TO YOU

1 Imagine you are at the scene in either photo **A** or **B**.
  a Write down three words to help you express how you might feel.
  b Write down three words to describe the things you might see around you.
  c What would you do next, and why?
  d Do the same for photo **D**. Explain how people can be positively and negatively affected by volcanoes.

2 Complete these sentences:
  a We know a volcano is active because …
  b Dormant volcanoes are those that …
  c Extinct volcanoes have …

3 Make a simple copy of photo **C**. Add the following labels (above right) where you think they fit best. (*Warning:* They can be placed in any part of the diagram!)

- I'm nowhere near the summit and I can smell sulphur.
- This ash has fallen 2 km from the volcano.
- From here you can see the lava bubbling.
- The temperature here measures 1200°C.
- Although this rock is molten it's not lava yet.
- This is the way the lava gets to the vent and crater above.
- The big volcanic bombs lie here, the smaller ones further away.

4 Use the following words to explain the journey of molten rock from deep in the Earth to become volcanic rock.

- eruption ● pipe ● magma ● vent ● ash
- lava ● basalt

What are the effects of a volcanic eruption?

Volcanic eruptions take many forms. As a result, volcanoes come in many different shapes.

The hot, runny **basalt** lavas which pour out from the Hawaiian shield volcanoes (diagram **D**) produce quite gentle slopes. The more viscous (sticky) **andesite** lava and ash that erupts from volcanoes like Etna in Sicily (Italy) produce steeper cone-shaped volcanoes (diagram **E**). Where the lavas are really thick (e.g. **rhyolite**), such as on Martinique in the Caribbean, steep-sided lava domes may form (diagram **F**).

A The Soufrière Hills Volcano, Montserrat

1992, January	Start of a series of earthquakes in southern Montserrat.
1994, June	One of the largest series of earthquakes experienced.
1995, 18 July	Chances Peak volcano erupts for the first time in 350 years. Thousands are forced to evacuate. Many take up temporary residence in 'safe areas' in the north, while others flee to neighbouring Caribbean islands, to New York and Britain.
August	Government declares a state of emergency.
December	Britain assists with rehabilitation programmes and grants millions of pounds in development aid.
1996, April	Britain announces that Montserratians will be granted residency and the right to work in the UK for up to two years.
1997, 25 June	Soufrière Hills volcano erupts with devastating effects. Two-thirds of the island is left uninhabitable and 19 people are killed. Plymouth, the capital, is abandoned. Montserrat's airport is closed, and the island is accessible only by helicopter or boat.
1998	Britain announces that Montserratians can apply for permanent residency.
2001, July	Eruption of the Soufrière Hills volcano causes widespread disruption.
2003, 12 July	Largest volcanic eruption since Chances Peak in 1995 destroys many buildings on the edge of the safe zone.
2004, 3 March	An explosion and collapse event lasts about 10 minutes. Pyroclastic flows reach the sea at the Tar River fan on at least two occasions.
2005, 3 July	Explosive eruption at 1.14 am follows a series of minor earthquakes. Ash cloud reaches 4500–6000 metres above the Earth.

B Timeline of Montserrat eruptions

Fantastic Facts

- Many geologists believe that a worldwide phase of volcanic eruptions 65 million years ago changed the atmosphere so violently that it led to the extinction of the dinosaurs.
- The Laki (Iceland) eruption in the 1780s was thought by American statesman Thomas Jefferson to have caused the severe, dark, cold winter he witnessed in France in 1783/84. Today it is believed that atmospheric pollution from that eruption caused 10 000 extra deaths in the UK at that time.
- Volcanic gases built up beneath lake-bed muds in Cameroon, Africa in 1986 until one night they leaked out and poured down a valley, killing 1700 people in their sleep.

C

12 July 2003

A University of Arkansas professor and his students had an unexpected close-up view of an erupting volcano as they conducted research this summer. They were working on the Caribbean island of Montserrat when the Soufrière Hills volcano erupted, about 5 km from where they were staying. During the day they could see clouds of ash and saw where the flows met the ocean. Geysers of water flashed upwards as the gas hit the ocean. Later a rainstorm turned the ash cloud into a mud bath. Driving home they couldn't clear the windscreen and one of the vehicles was hit by a mudslide. The big eruption occurred between 11 and 11.30 pm.

'You could hear rocks hitting the roof, which started leaking,' the students reported.

Everyone picked up pots to put on their heads for protection should the rocks start coming through the roof. Lightning produced by the ash clouds flashed continuously and the air smelled sulphurous. Finally, the eruption subsided and the students fell asleep around 3 am. The next day they awoke to a moon-like landscape, with everything covered in a uniform layer of grey ash. They saw residents resignedly digging themselves out from underneath another eruption that had dumped about 12.5 cm of ash in about 1 ¹/₂ hours.

'What was once lush and green was dead and looked like a war zone,' the professor said. 'It was as if we had travelled to another country overnight.'

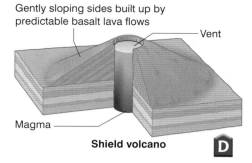

Gently sloping sides built up by predictable basalt lava flows — Vent — Magma

Shield volcano **D**

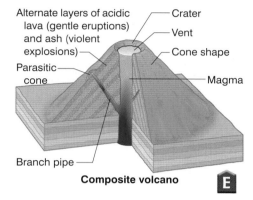

Alternate layers of acidic lava (gentle eruptions) and ash (violent explosions) — Crater — Vent — Cone shape — Magma — Parasitic cone — Branch pipe

Composite volcano **E**

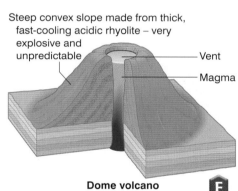

Steep convex slope made from thick, fast-cooling acidic rhyolite – very explosive and unpredictable — Vent — Magma

Dome volcano **F**

Remember ...

In *Horizons 1* Unit 6 'Exploring the UK' you looked at the variety of landscapes in the UK. Volcanic activity in the UK over 500 million years has produced such distinctive landforms as the Langdale Pikes in the Lake District, the Giant's Causeway in County Antrim and Arthur's Seat in Edinburgh. Find out when these features were created and why they now attract tourists (see *Horizons 2* Unit 6 'Tourism').

Key Words!

Basalt
Hot, runny lava that cools into very fine-grained, dark rock.

Andesite
Thicker, sticky lava that often produces explosive eruptions with clouds of ash.

Rhyolite
Very sticky lava and explosive eruptions.

OVER TO YOU

1 Read the text in timeline **B**.
  a Find five different problems caused by the eruption of the Montserrat volcano from 1995 onwards.
  b Which of these problems do you think are life-threatening?

2 From the account in resource **C**, identify some of the dangers of being in an eruption.

3 Take the parts of sentences below to make three complete sentences correctly describing the main forms of volcano.

4 Select one of the three volcanic types described in your answer to activity 3. Write a paragraph describing the possible effects of a volcanic eruption on the local inhabitants, ecosystem and economy.

Hint: Try to research an actual case study of that type of volcano, for example:
Shield ⟶ Mauna Loa, Hawaii
Cone ⟶ Mount Pinatubo
Dome ⟶ Martinique.

Form	Lava	Explanation
▲ Steep-sided volcanoes are often made from	● runny basalt lavas that can travel for miles,	■ so build up around the vent to form a dome.
▲ Shield volcanoes have gentle slopes because they are created by	● andesite lavas and ash from many eruptions,	■ which build up into a steep-sided cone shape.
▲ Composite volcanoes can be formed by layers of	● viscous rhyolite lavas that cannot travel far	■ leaving less lava to cool around the vent.

What can virtual volcanoes tell us?

Iceland and Montserrat (photos *A* and *B*) are both volcanic islands in the Atlantic Ocean, but there the similarity ends. There are important physical differences between them, in the types of volcanism they experience and in the way their populations are affected by regular eruptions. Fact file *C* tells us something about these countries, and you already know quite a lot about Montserrat, but you need to dig deeper.

Eruption in Iceland **A**

Comparing volcanism in Iceland and Montserrat

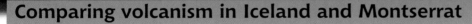

Using the web to search for information is a good way of accessing a lot of information quickly. However, not everything on the web is useful or reliable. You need to **critically evaluate** your sources.

- *Who* ... wrote it?
  Hint: Is that a reliable source?

- *Where* ... has it come from?
  Hint: Is it an 'official', commercial or amateur site?

- *Why* ... has it concentrated on certain aspects?
  Hint: Is it biased?

- *What* ... can this site tell you – and what can it *not* tell you – about your key questions?

- *When* ... was it written?
  Hint: When was it last updated? Is it up to date?

- *How* ... will you select only the information that is relevant and not just related to the points you are trying to make?

Help!

Comparing and contrasting

Comparing two items isn't the same as just listing their characteristics. It should involve you in:
- finding the similarities and the differences
- explaining why the differences occur
- explaining how these differences may be important.

To do this well you need to provide evidence (such as facts, figures and places) to support the points you make.

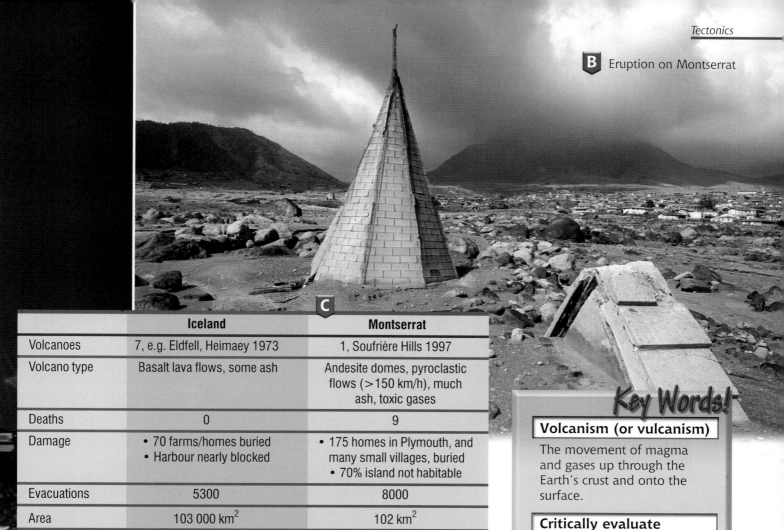

B Eruption on Montserrat

C

	Iceland	Montserrat
Volcanoes	7, e.g. Eldfell, Heimaey 1973	1, Soufrière Hills 1997
Volcano type	Basalt lava flows, some ash	Andesite domes, pyroclastic flows (>150 km/h), much ash, toxic gases
Deaths	0	9
Damage	• 70 farms/homes buried • Harbour nearly blocked	• 175 homes in Plymouth, and many small villages, buried • 70% island not habitable
Evacuations	5300	8000
Area	103 000 km²	102 km²
Country's wealth (GNP/person)	$31 900	$3400
Population	296 737	9341

Key Words!

Volcanism (or vulcanism)

The movement of magma and gases up through the Earth's crust and onto the surface.

Critically evaluate

To test the reliability of information and findings.

OVER TO YOU

1 Start your comparison by studying resources **A–C**. Use the information you gather from these sources to complete a Venn diagram like the one below.

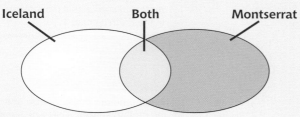

Iceland Both Montserrat

2 With a partner, make a list of which categories of information you will search for on both Iceland and Montserrat.

Hint: They might include: type of volcano, plate tectonic situation, history of eruption, death toll, cost, damage done, wealth of country, etc.

3 Plan your report or presentation, or use PowerPoint, to test this hypothesis:

'In dealing with eruptions, the type of volcanism is more important than the wealth of the country affected.'

You will need to include:
● an introduction to explain what you intend to do
● maps to show where these places are
● sections on Iceland and Montserrat:
  – background on size and economy
  – history of volcanism
  – damage caused
  – how it has been managed
  – any benefits, e.g. tourism, energy
● conclusion – if you find the hypothesis true or false, and why.

WEBLINKS **You will find links to websites on volcanism in Iceland and Montserrat at** www.nelsonthornes.com/horizons

How much can prediction and prevention help?

No place in the world is completely safe from natural hazards, but some are more prone to earthquakes and volcanoes than others.

In the USA, over 20 million people live in the San Francisco and Los Angeles areas. Both cities lie along the San Andreas Fault which can produce devastating earthquakes. Another 20 million people live within the shadow of the 'smoking mountain' Popacatepetl. It is North America's second biggest volcano, and lies just 70 km south-east of Mexico City.

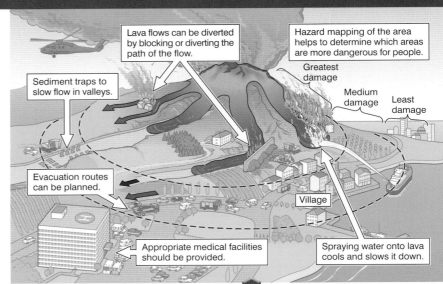

Lava flows can be diverted by blocking or diverting the path of the flow.

Hazard mapping of the area helps to determine which areas are more dangerous for people.

Sediment traps to slow flow in valleys.

Greatest damage

Medium damage

Least damage

Evacuation routes can be planned.

Village

Appropriate medical facilities should be provided.

Spraying water onto lava cools and slows it down.

B Preventing damage by a volcano

These places all have their attractions for people. But the threats in these areas mean that great efforts must be made to predict future events and plans made to reduce the damage when an earthquake or volcano does finally happen.

Other types of **remote sensing** from satellites can also indicate earth movements.

Global positioning satellites (GPS) can be used to sense minute changes in the position of the land near a fault line or a volcano.

Heat and gas emissions sensors detect changes in the magma beneath a volcano as it rises before an eruption.

Laser reflectors, tilt and creep meters record actual movements in the Earth's crust.

Seismometers measure how and when the ground shakes. These patterns can help predict earthquakes and may indicate that a volcanic eruption is likely.

A Methods of predicting earthquakes and volcanoes

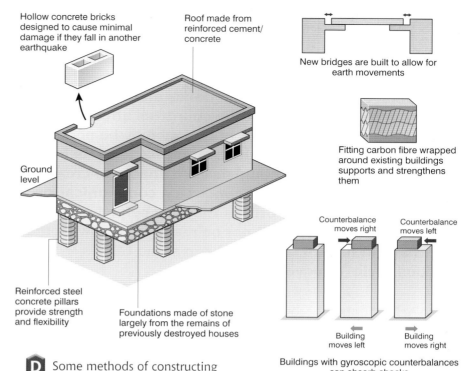

Hollow concrete bricks designed to cause minimal damage if they fall in another earthquake

Roof made from reinforced cement/concrete

New bridges are built to allow for earth movements

Fitting carbon fibre wrapped around existing buildings supports and strengthens them

Ground level

Reinforced steel concrete pillars provide strength and flexibility

Foundations made of stone largely from the remains of previously destroyed houses

Counterbalance moves right

Counterbalance moves left

Building moves left

Building moves right

Buildings with gyroscopic counterbalances can absorb shocks

D Some methods of constructing earthquake-proof buildings

C A building constructed to withstand earthquakes – the concrete beams soak up the shocks

OVER TO YOU

1 Imagine that your home is going to experience a major earthquake in 1 minute.

You have 10 seconds to think of five things you might grab from your home in a hurry.

Write down those things and compare your list with your partner's.

2 If the earthquake hit your home it must have hit the region – so it will now be devastated.
  a Which of your five items would help you to survive in the short term?
  b Which five items would help you to survive in the long term?
  c Which were just luxuries?
  d How would the following have helped you make better choices?

  - Planning ● Time ● Information
  - Advice ● Previous experience

Choose three of these and explain how they would help.

3 Study resources **A–D**. Which hazard prevention and prediction methods are the responsibility of the individual?

4 Which of the forms of prediction or prevention should be the responsibility of:
  a the local community
  b national government
  c international organisations?

Explain your answers.

5 Choose one of the following statements and use examples you have studied to explain why you agree or disagree with it.
  a 'Technology will not stop people dying from earthquakes and volcanoes.'
  b 'Tectonic events will become more predictable and will cause fewer deaths in the future.'

PASSPORT · PASSPORT

TO THE WORLD

If you wish to prepare yourself to help people in a practical way, you can study for a degree in Disaster Management at several UK universities.

How can aid reduce the damage?

The damage inflicted by earthquakes and volcanoes can often be so severe that the countries affected cannot cope. Huge amounts of money may be needed to repair damage and get the country back on its feet. At the same time such countries are unable to create the wealth required because industry, communications and trade are in ruins. Unless they are helped on the road to recovery they will not be ready to deal with the next natural hazard. This can keep some LEDCs in a 'vicious cycle' of poverty.

- Bury dead to avoid disease
- Fix roads and bridges
- Medical care
- Export goods to make money
- Feed and shelter homeless
- Build new homes
- Install early warning systems
- Get industry working again
- Find trapped people

Aid to help countries recover from disasters comes in many forms. From food to factories, different kinds of help are needed at different stages. It is given by individuals, charities, governments and international organisations (photo **C** and resource **D**).

All of these problems are **A** the effects of one earthquake. Which should be dealt with first?

Stage 1 Disaster occurs, destroying homes, communications, industry (especially farming).

Stage 4 Disaster strikes again at country that is weaker than it was before, and less able to recover.

Stage 2 Expense of rebuild – country has few ways of creating wealth, so puts country into debt.

Cycle

Aid programme relieves short-term problems and helps country back to economic independence.

broken

Stage 3 Little or no money left to build defences or warning systems against repeated natural disasters.

B Can the vicious cycle of poverty be broken by aid?

- **Emergency relief** – public and government money is raised quickly to help soon after a disaster occurs. Amounts depend on public reactions.

- **Voluntary aid** – private money is raised by charities, e.g. Oxfam, Cafod, Save the Children, World Relief. Their help ranges from short-term to longer-term projects.

- **Bilateral and multilateral aid** – bilateral aid is given by one country to another, and it is often 'tied' to conditions. Multilateral aid involves MEDCs giving money to organisations such as the World Bank or the International Monetary Fund (IMF), which can then help countries in difficulty. Many LEDCs hit by disaster owe money to the IMF, which in some cases may write off the debt. These organisations are involved in longer-term aid to help countries become more stable – but there can be conditions attached to that help.

C

Indonesian villagers look up to catch airdropped supplies. What is the most useful thing these survivors could receive?

D These are just some of the organisations that were involved in relief following the Indonesian tsunami 2004

---

1 What is aid and where does it come from?

2 Look at the points in resource **A**, which highlight some of the problems faced by countries like Indonesia after an earthquake or any natural disaster.
  a Write the points in the order in which you think they should be dealt with.
  b Select the first *three* items in your list and explain why you think they need to be dealt with immediately.
  c Decide which problems the country should be able to deal with mainly by itself, and shade those *green*. Identify those that will probably require a lot of external aid, and shade those *red*.
  d Explain why some problems may need aid from other countries.
  e What kind of aid should these countries provide, and when?

Hint: Money, trained staff, helicopters, medicines, construction equipment … etc.

3 Study diagram **B**.
  a Write a paragraph to explain why many people think aid can help to break the cycle of poverty suffered by disaster-prone countries.
  b Write another paragraph to explain why some people think aid will not solve the problems of these countries.

4 Find out about a world aid agency that contributed to the 2004/05 Indonesian tsunami aid programme (resource **D**). Write a report to explain how it helps countries to recover from the tsunami or other natural disasters. Present your work as a report or PowerPoint presentation, or make a video newscast.

OVER TO YOU

Links to… Pages 34–35 in this book, which tell you more about the work of aid organisations.

WEBLINKS You will find links to some aid agencies at www.nelsonthornes.com/horizons

You have been appointed as minister in charge of disaster relief in a country on the west coast of South America. Hazard Control Surveys have informed you that a volcanic event is likely within one year at Pico Magdalena in the western section of your province. The important agricultural towns of San Sebastian (population 3000) and Villa Solana (population 1500) lie at the foot of the volcano, close to the main highway and the railway connecting the capital, Peragua, with the major port of Pacifico.

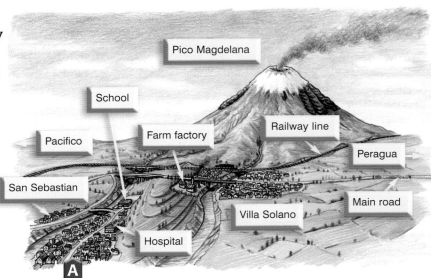

A

Life and death decisions?

You have been put in charge of reducing the impact of the eruption if it happens. You have a very limited budget (US$ 1 million) to spend, and only a small team of workers. Table **B** shows the cost of the various methods of prediction and precaution which you could use. You need to produce a report urgently, outlining for central government your intended prediction/precaution schemes. Don't go over budget!

Your final report must include:
- a brief description of the problem
- an annotated map showing exactly where you will locate/implement your chosen methods
- a table showing the methods you have chosen and the costs involved
- an explanation of how your scheme will work, and its limitations.

B Costs of methods of prediction and precaution

	US $ (thousands)	Symbol		US $ (thousands)	Symbol
Predictions			**Precautions – structural**		
Hazard mapping	10		Barrier walls (per km)	200	
Geophysical survey team (per year)	50		Diversionary lava channels	100	
Satellite monitoring (per year)	300				
Permanent observatory	500		**Precautions – behavioural**		
Precautions – emergency			Education/evacuation drills	5	
Damming lava channels – helicopter (per week)	200		Evacuation routes and warning systems	50	
Paramedic relief/rescue squad (per year)	500		New rest/relief centres	200	
Semi-trained volunteer rescue teams (per year)	100		Emergency food and water supplies	100	
Estimated cost to compensate businesses on evacuation (per month)	100		Relocate all inhabitants in new towns and re-route road and rail	3000	

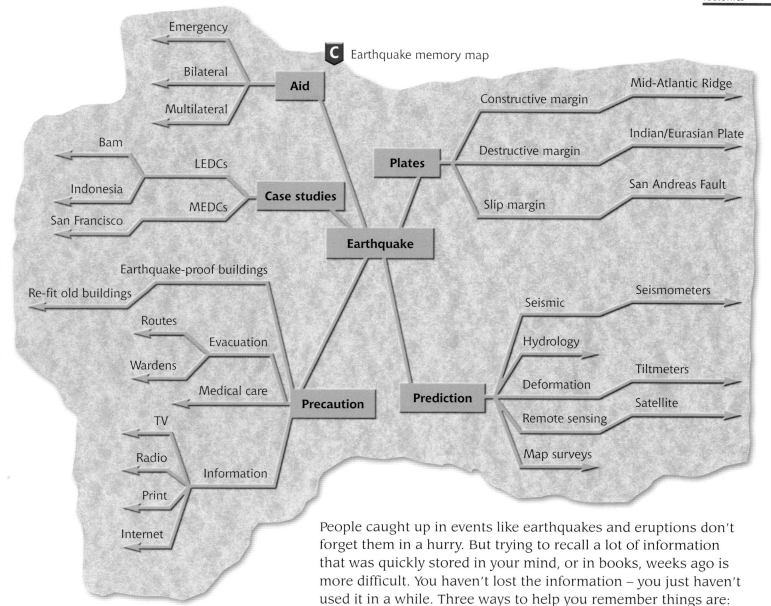

C Earthquake memory map

People caught up in events like earthquakes and eruptions don't forget them in a hurry. But trying to recall a lot of information that was quickly stored in your mind, or in books, weeks ago is more difficult. You haven't lost the information – you just haven't used it in a while. Three ways to help you remember things are:

- store things in an organised way
- mentally connect your thoughts or facts to a memorable image and/or colour
- link together the things you want to remember.

All of these things are made easier if you actively create a personal memory map of your own.

Mapping your memory

1 Study diagram **C**. It shows one pupil's memory map of what they learned in this unit about earthquakes. What could you add to make the memory map more complete?

Hint: Colours and pictures help us remember, and place names add useful detail.

2 Redraw the map for yourself on a full page of your notebook, placed sideways. Add your own extra information and simple diagrams, and select your own colours.

3 Draw another memory map, for either volcanoes, Earth structure, plate tectonics or aid.

OVER TO YOU

80:20

What is development?

Where are we going?

Development is a complex term. Most simply, development means all people reaching an acceptable standard of living, and having the basic things they need to live. Development is a never-ending process: people will always be striving to improve the quality of their lives and the lives of their children. In this unit you will consider development, and your role in the process.

In this unit you will learn about:

- **different definitions of development**
- **world poverty, its causes and why it is unevenly spread**
- **ways of using data to measure and analyse development patterns**
- **what governments, voluntary groups and individuals can do to support development**
- **the importance of sustainable development, and fair trade.**

A

A mere 12% of the world's population uses 85% of its water.

As many as 80% of the world's population live in poor countries. The rich countries, with only 20% of the population, control 80% of the global resources. This leaves the poor 80% of the population to get by on 20% of the world's resources. Poverty and uneven development are major world issues. People living in rich countries such as the United Kingdom generally have a good quality of life. This can make it difficult for us to imagine what life is like for the poor 80% of the world's population.

1.3 billion people (two-thirds of them women) of the world's 6 billion people live in poverty.

Poverty kills 30 000 people every day.

The development compass rose

The development compass rose (DCR) shown in diagram **B** will help you view development issues from a variety of points of view and to begin to understand some of the complexities involved. You can use it to think of questions on what you can see in photo **C**, for example. You can also use it to write descriptions.

The world's top 3 billionaires have wealth greater than that of *all* the least developed countries and their 600 million people.

N for Natural

These are questions about the **natural environment** – climate, landscape, relief, water – and how people interact with it.

Examples:
- Why have the people chosen to live in this place?
- Is the land flat enough for people to build homes?

W for Who decides?

These are questions about who is in charge, who is the decision maker, who is making decisions about changes.

Examples:
- Who is making decisions for these people?
- Do you think these people have a say?

E for Economic

These are questions about how people are making a living, money, wealth, poverty, trade, aid.

Examples:
- Are these people rich or poor?
- How are they earning a living?

S for Social

These are questions about people, their relationships, traditions, culture and the way they live.

Example:
- How do their traditions affect the way they live?

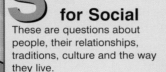

The development compass rose **B**

C

Nearly 1 billion people are illiterate.

More than 2.6 billion people do not have basic sanitation.

Half the population of Africa live on less than $1 a day.

1. Development is about making sure that people have the basic needs to live. What are these basic needs?

2. Why is this unit called '80:20'?

3. Read the facts about world poverty (photo **A**) carefully, and discuss them in a group.
   a. Which of the facts does your group find most shocking?
   b. Which facts highlight the uneven spread of world poverty?
   c. Use the internet to try to find out three more world poverty facts.

4. According to internationally accepted standards, anyone earning less than 60p (US $1) a day is living below the poverty line. Worldwide, 1.3 billion people live on less than $1 a day. Try to work out how much you and your family spend in a day.

5. a. Draw a development compass rose in the centre of a large sheet of paper.
   b. Write two questions for each point on your DCR about what you can see in photo **A** or **C**.
   c. Now work with a partner. First compare your questions, and then use the key questions for each point on the DCR to describe what photo **A** or **C** shows.

6. Turn to photo **D** on page 33 and repeat activity 5.

7. Compare your analysis of the two photos. Write lists of similarities and differences for each DCR point.

Where in the world?

Key Words!

To understand development we need to investigate patterns across the world. All countries are different, and we already know that world development patterns are uneven. Data is collected for every country in the world and can be mapped, as on map **A**. Interpreting this map will provide an opportunity to improve your place knowledge of the world.

Measuring development is not straightforward. There is much debate among geographers about what data makes a relevant and reliable indicator to show how developed a country is. The most common way is to focus on wealth. One indicator that is often used by geographers is **Gross Domestic Product (GDP)** per capita, or per person (map **A**).

Gross Domestic Product (GDP)

This is the value of all goods and services produced within a nation in a given year, divided by the total number of people living in that country. This figure is always measured in US dollars (US$), to make comparisons between countries easier.

(9)

NORTH AMERICA

Many different terms are used to describe rich and poor groups of countries **A**

Pacific Ocean

OVER TO YOU

1 a Use an atlas to help you to name the countries labelled 1–10 on map **A**.

   b Complete a copy of table **B**. List the 10 countries in order of wealth, giving the richest first.

No.	Country	Continent	GDP per capita	MEDC or LEDC
1				
2				
3				

B

2 Why is the GDP figure for every country in US$, even though they all have their own currencies?

3 Name five other countries in the same GDP bands as countries 2 and 7.

4 Compare the world pattern of GDP with the North–South line. Does the line match the patterns of wealth shown on the map?

5 Write a paragraph describing the distribution of each of the four income groups of countries shown on map **A**.

6 Look carefully at all the resources on these two pages. Identify some of the disadvantages of using GDP as an indicator of development.

The Third World
This is an old term used to describe the groups of poor countries. Originally the First World countries were the Western nations, and the Second World was the old Soviet bloc.

KEY
GDP per capita, 2004 (US$)
- Low income: 755 or less
- Lower middle income: 756–2995
- Upper middle income: 2996–9265
- High income: 9266 or more

Rank	Country	Population (millions)
1	China	1306
2	India	1080
3	USA	297
4	Indonesia	242
5	Brazil	186
6	Pakistan	162
7	Bangladesh	144
8	Russia	143
9	Nigeria	129
10	Japan	127

World's top ten countries: population, 2005

North–South Line
The line on the map divides the world into two halves: the rich North and the poor South. This division was first suggested in 1980. It can be confusing, though, because some rich countries are in the southern hemisphere and some poor countries are in the northern hemisphere.

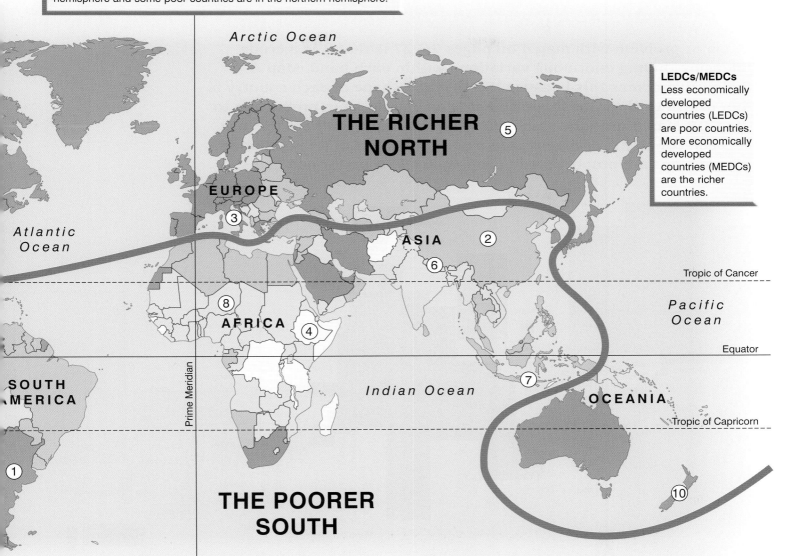

LEDCs/MEDCs
Less economically developed countries (LEDCs) are poor countries. More economically developed countries (MEDCs) are the richer countries.

Country	GDP per capita (US$)	Population (thousands)
Luxembourg	48 309	469
USA	35 992	297 753
Bermuda	34 893	65
San Marino	33 429	29
Norway	32 797	4593
Switzerland	31 891	7489
Cayman Islands	30 286	44
Iceland	30 071	297
Belgium	29 128	10 364
Canada	29 003	32 805

World's top ten countries: GDP per capita, 2005 **D**

Country	GDP per capita (US$)	Population (thousands)
East Timor	441	1040
Mayotte	476	194
Sierra Leone	493	6017
Burundi	516	6371
Somalia	532	8592
Tanzania	568	36 766
Gaza Strip	576	1376
Malawi	585	12 159
Congo, Dem. Rep.	600	60 086
Afghanistan	662	29 929

World's bottom ten countries: GDP per capita, 2005 **E**

How do we measure development?

A major problem with map *A* on pages 26–27 is that it is a crude measure, hiding enormous variations within each band. Map *A* below overcomes this because the size and shape of each country is not drawn to show its shape and area as usual, but in proportion to its GDP. Map *B* uses the same mapping technique but here the size of each country is drawn in proportion to the size of its population. These maps are proportional or topologically transformed maps.

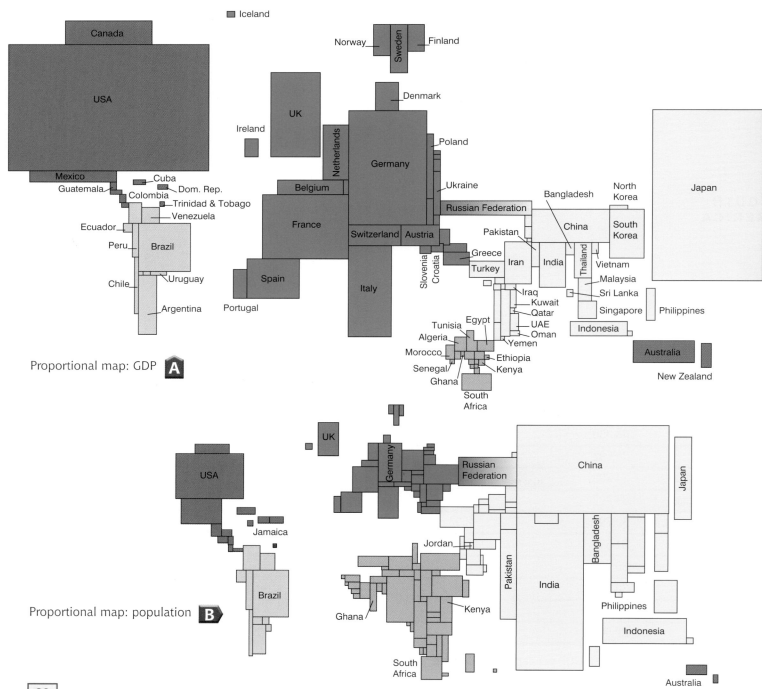

Proportional map: GDP **A**

Proportional map: population **B**

Development is much more than investigating the wealth of a country. (Look back at your work on the development compass rose on pages 24–25.) This is why many geographers are unhappy about relying on GDP per capita as a development indicator. In 1990 the United Nations created its own measure of development, called the **Human Development Index (HDI)**. Each year the UN produces a Human Development Report using that index.

WEBLINKS

You will find a link to the latest Human Development Report at
www.nelsonthornes.com/horizons

Key Words!

Human Development Index (HDI)

It is used by the United Nations to measure development, using a combination of measures: life expectancy, education, and income per capita. The index has a value between 0 and 1. The higher the value, the higher the level of human development.

Human Development Index **C**

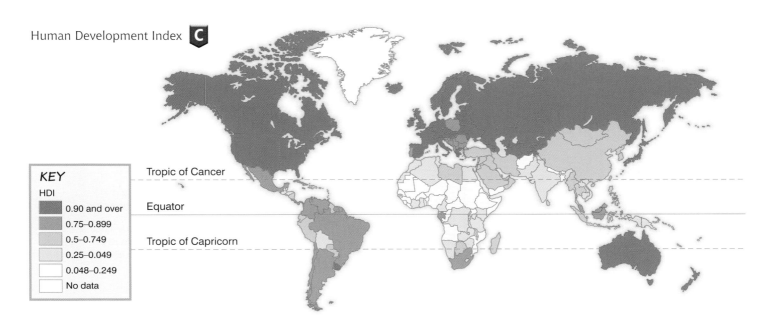

KEY

HDI

- 0.90 and over
- 0.75–0.899
- 0.5–0.749
- 0.25–0.049
- 0.048–0.249
- No data

Tropic of Cancer

Equator

Tropic of Capricorn

OVER TO YOU

1 What is a topologically transformed map?

2 Compare map **A** with map **A** on pages 26–27. Both maps show GNP, but which map gives you a clearer understanding of the distribution of GNP?

Hint: Compare Switzerland and Portugal on the two maps.

3 Each continent of the world is shaded a different colour on the transformed map **A**. What do you notice about the size of each continent according to their share of GDP compared with their area?

4 Which countries and continents surprise you on map **A**?

5 Write a rank order list of the top ten most developed countries using map **A**.

6 Compare maps **A** and **B**. How are the continents and countries different on these maps?

7 What development issues can you identify from these differences?

8 What is the HDI?

9 Why do many geographers think that the HDI is a better measure of development than GDP?

10 Use map **C** to describe the distribution of countries with:
   a the highest HDI (over 0.90)
   b the lowest HDI (under 0.25).

11 Go to the Human Development Report website and download the latest report that lists countries according to their HDI. Write a rank order list of the top ten and bottom ten countries. Compare these with lists **D** and **E** for GDP on page 27. Identify any differences and try to explain them.

How do you use ICT for a development enquiry?

In this unit so far you have investigated ways of measuring development using data and maps. ICT can be useful in this process, allowing you to analyse statistical data quickly to identify geographical patterns. You can either select your own countries and data sets for a measuring development enquiry, or use the data provided below.

Remember ...

In *Horizons 1* Unit 5 'Work' pages 102–103, you investigated world development, grouping countries according to employment structure and *Gross National Income* (GNI).
In *Horizons 2* you used ICT in the 'Weather' enquiry process on pages 56–57.

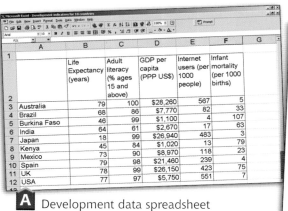

A Development data spreadsheet

	Life Expectancy (years)	Adult literacy (% ages 15 and above)	GDP per capita (PPP US$)	Internet users (per 1000 people)	Infant mortality (per 1000 births)
Australia	79	100	$28,260	567	5
Brazil	68	86	$7,770	82	33
Burkina Faso	46	99	$1,100	4	107
India	64	61	$2,670	17	63
Japan	18	99	$26,940	483	3
Kenya	45	84	$1,020	13	79
Mexico	73	90	$8,970	118	23
Spain	79	98	$21,460	239	4
UK	78	99	$26,150	423	75
USA	77	97	$5,750	551	7

World Bank GIS website **C**

4 Click on this tab to view results selected.

3 Click on these tabs to select data and year.

2 Selected countries will appear here.

1 Click on countries and then scroll down to select button.

Step 1

Preparing the investigation

The key question for this investigation is:
- How do I determine the least developed country?

To investigate this question it is necessary to select countries and different types of data. This has already been done for you in spreadsheet **A**.

1 a Make a copy of the table below and then in the first column enter each country shown on spreadsheet **A**.
 b Each of these countries is numbered on map **B**. Use an atlas to help you complete the second column of your table, using the numbers from the map.
 c In the third column name the continent in which each country is located.

Country	Location on map *B*	Continent	MEDC or LEDC

 d In the fourth column record whether the country is in an MEDC or LEDC.

2 a Discuss with a partner whether the countries provided in the list on spreadsheet **A** represent a good sample of the world for investigation.
 b Discuss how you could further improve the sample.

3 Identify ten different countries for investigation. Explain the criteria you have used for your selection.

4 Look carefully at the five indicators of development that have been used in spreadsheet **A**.
 a Explain what each indicator is measuring.
 b Draw a development compass rose like the one on page 25. Write each of the indicators where you think it fits on the rose.
 c Discuss with a partner where you could obtain your own development data for countries.
 d Identify five different indicators of development for investigation. Make sure that all the elements of the development compass rose are represented.

Presenting your findings

8 Use the sort facility of the spreadsheet to rank the countries for each data set.

9 Use the chart wizard in the spreadsheet to create charts for each indicator, with the data sorted into rank order.

Analysing the results

10 Write a description for each development indicator.

> **Tips for your write-up**
>
> ● Word-process your analysis, and copy and paste your charts into your work. Use the software tools to label the patterns shown on the charts.
>
> ● Describe and compare each development indicator. Look for patterns – for example: Do the countries have the same rank order for each indicator? Are there any anomalies?

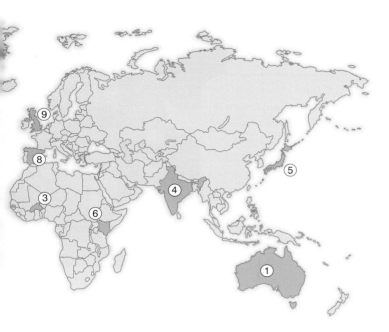

Reaching a conclusion

11 a Insert a second column for each set of data in your spreadsheet, to enter the ranking for each country.

b Type in the rank score for each country for each data set. The most developed will score 1 and the least developed 10.

c Insert a 'Total' column. Create a formula to total the ranking scores for each country. Again, the total column can be sorted using the spreadsheet tools to determine the level of development for each country.

d Create a chart for this data.

12 Write a paragraph explaining what the chart shows, and to answer your key questions.

Collecting information

5 You can either use the data provided in spreadsheet **A** to conduct this enquiry, or collect your own from one of the following sources:

● an online Geographical Information System (GIS), for example the World Bank data query website shown in **C**

● GIS software that may be available on your school's computer network

● the data pages in a school atlas.

You could collect data for the countries and indicators you identified in step 1.

6 Record your information carefully. Export the development indicators into a spreadsheet like the one in **A**.

7 It is important that your data is accurate if you are to reach meaningful conclusions. Some of the data on spreadsheet **A** is inaccurate.

a Look carefully at the data in **A** and identify the wrong data.

b Explain your choices and suggest the correct values. Your teacher will be able to provide you with the correct data.

Evaluating your work

13 Suggest ways you could have improved your data collection. For example, was your choice of countries and development indicators suitable for your investigation?

14 Discuss with a partner how this investigation has improved your understanding of development.

You will find a link to the World Bank GIS website, and others, at www.nelsonthornes.com/horizons

What are the causes of poverty?

This quote from Nelson Mandela's speech hints at some of the underlying causes of world poverty. See if you can spot them, and match them to photos *B–E*.

Photos **B–E** represent some of the main causes of world poverty.

Speech made by Nelson Mandela in Norway, 6 November 2004 **A**

Today we live in a world that is divided. A world in which we have made great progress and advances in science and technology. But it is also a world where millions of children die because they have no access to medicines. We live in a world where knowledge and information have made enormous strides, yet millions of children are not in school… It is a world of great promise and hope. It is also a world of despair, disease and hunger…

What are the real causes of poverty?

Debt
Many LEDCs borrowed money from MEDCs and the World Bank in the 1970s when interest rates were low. They hoped to use the money to develop, but interest rates have increased. Now the poor countries can't afford to pay back the interest on their loans, never mind the loans themselves. Some countries have to pay more in interest than they can spend on health and education.

Unfair trade
LEDCs are penalised by unfair trade agreements, a lack of technology and investment, and rapidly changing prices for their goods. In many LEDCs the main employment is farming. With little industry, most developing countries have few high-value goods to export. Most exports from LEDCs are low-cost primary goods such as cocoa, coffee or bananas. If they do have higher-value goods to export, such as manufactured products – cars and washing machines, for example – they often find that MEDCs set up trade barriers to protect their own industries.

B

C

Wars
When a country is at war (including civil war), basic services like education and healthcare are disrupted. People leave their homes as refugees. Crops are destroyed. Companies will not risk spending millions of pounds setting up a factory in an unstable country if it is likely to be destroyed in a war.

Health/disease
Poor people often do not have access to sewage disposal or clean water, and so are much more likely to suffer illness and disease. They often lack the means to obtain the healthcare they need. They are also often uninformed on how they can avoid risks. Poverty is a major factor in the spread of HIV/AIDS in many parts of Africa.

F World poverty facts

1	In the UK only 2% of people are employed in agriculture. In India 67% of the workforce is employed in agriculture.
2	The world's poorest countries still owe £190 billion to rich countries.
3	20 of the world's 38 poorest countries are experiencing an armed conflict, or did so very recently.
4	More than 40% of women in Africa do not have access to basic education.
5	In 2000, the Zambian government spent £9.80 per person on healthcare and £13.30 per person on annual debt repayments.
6	The World Health Organisation estimates that 80% of all sickness in the world can be blamed on unsafe water and poor sanitation.
7	Around the world, a total of 114 million children do not get even a basic education.
8	More than 2.6 billion people – over 40% of the world's population – do not have basic sanitation, and more than 1 billion people still use unsafe sources of drinking water.
9	It is estimated that of a global workforce of 3 billion people, 140 million are unemployed, and between a quarter and a third are underemployed.

D

E

Nature
Areas such as the Sahara have a very dry climate. Soils tend to be poor, it is difficult to grow crops and there is always the danger of famine. Many LEDCs have few natural resources to export or to attract industry. In mountainous regions it can be difficult to farm, and expensive to build roads. Some countries regularly experience natural disasters.
(Remember Bangladesh: *Horizons 1* pages 76–81.)

The low status of women
In many LEDCs women do not have equal rights, and do not have access to education. Countries waste 50% of their human resources. Women have a vital role to play in development.

Education
Without education it is difficult to escape poverty. Poor people cannot afford to send their children to school. If the adults in the family cannot earn enough to live on, children may have to work rather than go to school.

OVER TO YOU

1 Discuss with a partner the key message that Nelson Mandela was trying to communicate in his speech.

2 **a** Write a list of the major causes of poverty.
b Match the poverty facts in table **F** to each cause. Write each fact under the relevant cause in your list.
c Match photos **B–E** to each cause. Write the letter for each photo next to the relevant cause in your list.
d Link photo **D** on page 109 to a cause.

3 Draw a development compass rose. Write each of the causes where you think it fits on the rose.

4 Look carefully at map **A** on pages 26–27 and back cover map **F**. Write a list of the LEDCs that you think are poor because of their natural or physical geography.

5 **a** Draw a concept map like diagram **G** to help you find connections between the main causes of world poverty.

G

Debt	Unfair trade
Ill-health and disease	Status of women
War	Education

b Write a label on each connection to explain the link.
c Colour in *red* the lines that you think form the main connections.
d Discuss with a partner what you think are the three main causes of poverty. Shade these boxes *red*.

6 Working in groups of four, each take one of the photos **B–E**. Write down your answers to the 5W questions for your photo, then swap photos and compare your answers.

5W questions: *What? Where? When? Why? Who?*

33

80:20 – What can be done?

Many people all over the world are now aware of the issues of poverty. Pressure is increasingly put on world leaders to act to relieve the suffering, and to change the 80:20 balance between the rich and the poor.

In September 2000, world leaders responded to pressure in a very positive way. At the start of a new century they agreed a set of goals for the world to meet by 2015 (resource **A**).

Links to... Investigating this world issue links to global citizenship.

A

UNITED NATIONS

The Millennium Development Goals (MDGs) – a set of eight goals that aim to halve world poverty by:

1. Halving the proportion of people who suffer from extreme hunger and of people living on less than $1 (60p) a day.

2. Achieving universal primary education.

3. Getting rid of gender inequalities in primary and secondary education, preferably by 2005 and at all levels by 2015.

4. Reducing by two-thirds the mortality rate among children under 5.

5. Reducing by three-quarters the ratio of women dying in childbirth.

6. Combating the spread of HIV and AIDS, and the incidence of malaria and other major diseases.

7. Ensuring environmental sustainability: reducing by half the proportion of people without access to safe drinking water and reversing the loss of environmental resources.

8. Securing a global partnership for development, working together on debt, trade, public health, aid and technology issues to promote economic growth and poverty reduction.

B

The campaign manifesto
'World poverty is sustained not by chance or nature, but by a combination of factors: injustice in global trade; the huge burden of debt; and insufficient and ineffective aid.'

Born in Kenya, Naima is the youngest of six children. Her mother, a brother and a sister die of malaria. (Another sister will later die of AIDS.) Their father looks after the remaining children on the family farm.

A new road, funded by aid, is built to the nearest town. This means that the village is no longer isolated. Naima's father now has access to a market to sell produce from the farm. Naima's sister can get a job in the nearby town. The family are now well fed.

Despite the promises of world leaders, it was clear in 2005 – a third of the way through the period – that the goals would not be met. In 2005 a world summit was held in Edinburgh of the G8, the leaders of the eight richest countries in the world. The 'Make Poverty History' campaign tried to sway public opinion to pressure these leaders into action to meet the Millennium Development Goals. This campaign brought together over 400 organisations from all over the world, including charities such as Comic Relief, Oxfam and Christian Aid. The campaign ended with Live 8 concerts during the weekend before the G8 summit on 8 July.

WEBLINKS You will find links to the Millennium Development Goals and the 'Make Poverty History' websites at www.nelsonthornes.com/horizons

2005   2006

1 Look at the MDGs in resource **A**.

a Discuss them with a partner and then arrange them in order of importance, with the one you think is the most important first.

b Explain your chosen order of goals.

c Look back at the causes of poverty outlined on pages 32–33. Which of these causes are being tackled by the MDGs?

d The MDGs have a total of 18 targets to be met by 2015. Find out about these on the Millennium Development Goals website.

2 a What did the 'Make Poverty History' campaign of 2005 hope to achieve?

b What is the G8? Find out which countries are members of the group.

c Look back at page 21. What sort of aid is the 'Make Poverty History' campaign offering LEDCs?

d Visit the 'Make Poverty History' website and compile a short report outlining the aims of the campaign and the methods used to achieve those aims.

3 Look carefully at timeline **C**.

a Create a biography summarising Naima's life story.

b At each key stage, aid will help to improve Naima's life. Copy and complete the following table to show how aid, and MDGs, will help Naima at each stage.

Year	Naima's age	Impact of aid on Naima's life	How MDGs will help Naima

c Create an alternative biography for Naima, showing what will happen if she does *not* have the support of aid.

d Look back at the previous pages in this unit. Which of the causes of poverty are being addressed and will lead to an improved quality of life for Naima?

OVER TO YOU

How it *could* be for Naima, born in **C** Kenya in 2005

Just $70 is how much it would cost in aid per African per year to help the continent this century. This is how aid could change the life of an imaginary Kenyan, Naima ...

Naima is immunised at a new clinic in the town. When she was born, 12% of infants under 5 died in Kenya. The average life expectancy for women was 47, but now Naima is likely to live to 72.

Naima's father is able to dry his surplus banana crop and has earned enough money to buy equipment to package the dried bananas. He can sell them at home and abroad, as trade barriers have been lifted. This allows Kenyan farmers to get a better price for their produce. Naima and her brother have free primary education. Their father can now afford to pay for their secondary education.

Naima starts her clinical training with consultants who have returned to Kenya after working abroad. When Naima was a child, there was 1 doctor for 100 000 people – now there is 1 doctor for 2000 people.

Alice, Naima's daughter, is a university lecturer in Nairobi. Alice sets up a second home in the family village, where she adopts the old customs and tries to instill traditional African values in her own two children. Naima has retired and lives in the village. She helps her grandchildren to learn about the best of old Africa, while living a totally different life from the one she had at birth.

Naima graduates with a medical degree from Nairobi University.

80:20 – What can *I* do?

Two of the Millennium Development Goals you investigated on pages 34–35 are related to education. Look back and see what they are.

Education is an important component of development, but many people in LEDCs do not have access to it. There are a number of reasons for this. Education costs money – for teachers, buildings and resources. Even when education is provided free by the state, there are still costs, such as uniforms, books, exam fees and transport. Families living in poverty have to make difficult choices. If the adults in the family cannot earn enough to live on, children may have to work rather than go to school. Many LEDCs are heavily in debt. They have had to cut the amount they spend on education to pay the interest on their loans.

Mkwakwani is a primary school in a poor rural area in Ukunda, on the outskirts of Mombasa in Kenya. The school was started in 1984 by the village community, which pays for the upkeep and running of the school.

In 2001 Suzanne Mehmet, a hairdresser from Scarborough, North Yorkshire, and her husband went on holiday to Kenya and stayed in Ukunda. During their stay they became friendly with one of the local boys and visited the school.

> The building was falling down around them. There was no electricity, water supply or sanitation. Most of the children sat on the floor for their lessons, as there were very few desks. The floor consisted of sand and rubble. Pencils were shared and treated like sacred possessions. Rocks were used as makeshift desks. The poverty was appalling. After returning from our holiday my husband and I were determined to help the school and its children. We set up the Mkwakwani School Charity. We began by sponsoring individual students but wanted ultimately to rebuild the school, provide water, electricity, sanitation – all the things we take for granted.

Suzanne Mehmet,
a Scarborough hairdresser **A**

From this... **B**

C ...to this

D Omari Pofu, headteacher of Mkwakwani School

> Although education is now free in Kenya, all teaching resources, buildings and uniforms still need to be paid for by the community. It cannot afford to pay, which is why the school was in a very poor state. We are relying entirely on the effort of Suzanne and her friends in changing the learning environment of our school. Suzanne is a rare gift from God who was brought to save us. She approached Raincliffe School in Scarborough, which agreed to twin with us, and raised over £4800 to rebuild classrooms – we now have 21. They also provided stationery, so owning a pen is no longer a problem for our pupils. The school now has 6 flush toilets and a well. We also have 600 desks – almost enough for all of our pupils to sit in pairs.

From the *Scarborough Evening News*, 18 June 2005 **E**

Three Rs will help to light up Kenyan pupils

Raincliffe School is calling for people to take part in a sponsored 'run, row and ride to Kenya' to raise money for an electricity supply to Mkwakwani School.

The school raised £5000 during Red Nose Day for the 'Light Up Kenya' appeal, which is part of the Mkwakwani School project run by Scarborough hairdresser Suzanne Mehmet.

After the school had raised half the cash needed with its Comic Relief events, staff decided to do something else to raise the remaining £5000.

Bob Chisholm, the school's Citizenship Coordinator, said, 'My colleagues, pupils and I kicked around a few ideas and estimated that the distance overland from Raincliffe to Kenya was about 5000 miles and we thought that between us we could run, row or ride the distance raising £1 per mile.'

Raincliffe School

Links to... We are all global citizens. Taking part in fund-raising activities to help pupils in LEDCs is also part of your Citizenship studies.

F Bob Chisholm, Raincliffe School's Citizenship Coordinator

Pupils, parents and staff have now raised over £10 000 since 2001 for the Mkwakwani School Project. As well as raising money for classrooms, we have also collected and sent out parcels of books, pens, pencils, paper and school shirts. We regularly link a mobile phone to our PA system so that Omari Pofu, Mkwakwani School's headteacher, can talk to our staff and pupils in school assembly. Once the money is raised for electricity, we would like to sponsor a video-conferencing link between the two schools so that staff and pupils can share life experiences.

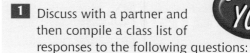

OVER TO YOU

1 Discuss with a partner and then compile a class list of responses to the following questions:
 a What would be the consequences for you, your families and your community if you were not able to go to school?
 b Why do so many children in poor countries not go to school?

2 **a** Education costs money. Working in groups of four, try to identify the major things on which your school spends money.
 b Make a class list of the most expensive items needed to run your school.
 c Try to find out how much it costs to run your school each year.

3 **a** Look again at the information about Mkwakwani School. Make a list of what you think are the most important spending priorities for this school.
 b How are these spending priorities different from those at your school?

4 Imagine you are a newspaper reporter. Your editor has asked you to write a 200-word report about the Mkwakwani School Project: its aims, how it developed, and what it has achieved. You could include quotes from key people in your report, and explain how the project helps to achieve the Millennium Development Goals.

5 Raincliffe School's latest fund-raising scheme is shown in newspaper article **E**. Your class could use this as a starting point to set up your own campaign to support a school in an LEDC, which will help achieve the Millennium Development Goals for education.

You could:
● Make a presentation to your year group in a school assembly, outlining how to support a school in an LEDC.
● Design posters and leaflets to promote the campaign, using DTP software, and display them around your school.

WEBLINKS **There are links to help you find out more about the Mkwakwani School Project, and other ways of supporting schools in LEDCs, at** www.nelsonthornes.com/horizons

Fair trade?

Any one country cannot produce and provide everything that its population wants or needs. To satisfy these needs, countries trade with one another. Trade connects us with millions of people across the world, producing the things we buy and use every day. Trade makes countries interdependent. Unfortunately, not every country gets a fair deal from trade.

World trade, often called free trade, could be a powerful force to reduce poverty, but the rules that govern it are biased in favour of the rich. The richer countries give their own farmers large amounts of money, called **subsidies**. This means they can sell their produce at lower prices. Farmers in poor countries cannot compete, and so they lose money and become poorer. LEDCs find it hard to sell manufactured goods to MEDCs. The MEDCs charge high taxes on these goods in order to keep them out – protecting their own industries. Poor countries produce most of the coffee, cocoa, cotton and copper that the rich world consumes – but the rich world sets the price, which is falling. The rich world buys cheap cotton and cocoa and turns these into expensive clothes and chocolate – so taking all of the profit.

But what can you do? Surely it's beyond your control? Wrong. You can buy Fairtrade products.

Fairtrade is an alternative approach to international trade. It is a growing, international movement which ensures that producers in poor countries get a fair deal – it *isn't* a charity. Farming is a risky business: when prices drop it can mean disaster for farmers. If they earn less than it costs to run the farm, they face real hardship, struggling to buy food and to keep their children in school. They may even lose their land and their livelihood. By buying Fairtrade products, you can provide a chance for farmers to sell their goods at a stable price. This covers their costs and means they can support their families and invest in a better future.

Fantastic Facts

- More than 40% of the world's population live in low-income countries – yet these countries account for just 3% of world trade.
- In Africa, a 1% increase in the share of world trade would generate $70 billion – five times what the continent gets in aid.
- For every dollar given to poor countries in aid, they lose two dollars to rich countries because of unfair trade barriers against their exports.
- A Ghanaian cocoa farmer gets only 1.2% of the price we pay for a bar of chocolate.

B

FAIRTRADE: HIGH STANDARDS GREAT PRODUCTS REAL CHANGE

The **FAIRTRADE Mark** is an independent consumer label which appears on products as **a guarantee that disadvantaged producers** are getting a better deal. Today, more than 5 million farmers, workers and their families across 49 developing countries benefit from the **international Fairtrade system**.

The Fairtrade Foundation is an **independent body** that awards the FAIRTRADE Mark to products which meet international Fairtrade standards.

You can find **hundreds of great quality** Fairtrade products in stores now – and the range is growing every day.

OUR FRUIT TASTES GREAT, BUT IN THE FAIRTRADE SYSTEM IT'S NOT ENOUGH JUST TO PRODUCE QUALITY. THIS FRUIT IS ALSO ABOUT THE WAY IT'S PRODUCED. IT'S ABOUT THE ENVIRONMENT. IT'S ABOUT A FAIR SYSTEM.
BERNARDO JAÉN, PINEAPPLE FARMER, COSTA RICA

CHECK OUT FAIRTRADE
YOUR **ONE MINUTE** GUIDE TO THE FAIRTRADE MARK:

Q: WHAT DOES THE FAIRTRADE MARK DO?
A: The FAIRTRADE Mark is unique: it guarantees farmers in developing countries a fair price for their products which covers their costs. Because this price is stable it allows them to plan for their future.

Q: WHY DO WE NEED IT?
A: The rules and practices of international trade are biased in favour of rich countries and powerful companies, often to the cost of poor producers. Buying Fairtrade certified products changes the lives of millions of people worldwide and shows how trade can be made to work in favour of poor people and the environment.

Q: HOW DOES IT WORK?
A: When you buy a product carrying the FAIRTRADE Mark, you know it has been independently certified to meet standards set by the Fairtrade Foundation. We check to make sure producers really are getting a better deal.

Q: IS IT A BRAND?
A: No. You can find the FAIRTRADE Mark on products from more than a hundred different companies. The FAIRTRADE Mark is an independent stamp of approval.

Guarantees **a better deal** for Third World Producers
FAIRTRADE

Guarantees **a better deal** for Third World Producers
AIRTRADE

CHECK OUT THE GROWING RANGE OF FAIRTRADE PRODUCTS
CHECK OUT FAIRTRADE AT SUPERMARKETS, INDEPENDENT RETAILERS, CAFES, RESTAURANTS, HOTELS, AT WORK, AT SCHOOL AND THROUGH CATERING SUPPLIERS...

WEBLINKS | **You will find a link to the Fairtrade website at** www.nelsonthornes.com/horizons

---

OVER TO YOU

1 What is world trade?

2 Read the 'Fantastic Facts'. What do they suggest about world trade?

3 Cartoon **A** presents a viewpoint about world trade.
  a Discuss the cartoon with a partner.
  b What is the cartoon saying about free trade?
  c Who are the characters in the cartoon?

4 Look carefully at resource **B**. It is from a Fairtrade information booklet.
  a What is Fairtrade?
  b What is the Fairtrade mark and what does it indicate?
  c What are the benefits of Fairtrade for the producer?
  d Write a list of the Fairtrade product range.
  e Which is the only product in the range that is not food or flowers?

5 Your class could help people in LEDCs in a variety of ways:
  ● Make sure that your family purchases Fairtrade products.
  ● Visit your local supermarket and carry out a survey. How many Fairtrade products does it stock, and how many brands?
  ● Set up a Fairtrade tuck shop, selling Fairtrade snacks at breaks and dinner times.
  ● Visit the Fairtrade website and download resources to create a Fairtrade exhibition, as part of a campaign to raise awareness in your school.

What is sustainable development?

The term *sustainable development* is frequently used in geography. In 1992 the *Earth Summit*, held in Rio de Janeiro in Brazil, agreed a blueprint for sustainable development. This action plan is called Agenda 21. It focuses on environmental, social and economic issues and how they inter-relate. National governments and local authorities are now required to develop strategies for sustainability that consider these three components.

Remember ...

Go back and re-read *Horizons 2* 'Passport to the World' pages 124–125. What issues about sustainability did you identify over the summer?

Development does not always bring benefits. Short-term economic gain, providing jobs and income for people, can have long-term costs for both people and the environment. According to one recent study, people are consuming the Earth's resources at a rate that is 20% faster than it can replenish itself. The findings of the most comprehensive environmental survey of the planet, the Millennium Ecosystem Assessment, were published in 2005. It concluded that the way society has sourced its food, fresh water, timber, fibre and fuel over the past 50 years has seriously degraded the environment. This was threatening the Earth's ability to sustain future generations, and undermining the Millennium Development Goals.

Development does not mean every person on the planet aspiring to own a car, fly halfway around the world on holiday and get a new mobile phone every year – we don't have enough Earth for this sort of unsustainable approach. In principle, sustainable development means not using up resources faster than the Earth can replenish them but rather 'treating the Earth as if we intended to stay'. It is about the interaction and interdependence of society, economy and the environment for present and future generations.

Links to... You have already studied sustainable development projects in *Horizons 2* pages 72–73 and pages 120–121. You will go on to investigate sustainable development projects in *Horizons 3* pages 92–95 and pages 96–101.

Sustainable or unsustainable?

1 What is sustainable development?

2 Why is sustainable development so important to the future of the planet and all of its inhabitants?

3 a Make a copy of diagram **I**.
b Label each section of your diagram to show the social, economic and environmental factors that need to be considered in sustainable development projects.

SOCIAL **I**

ECONOMIC

ENVIRONMENTAL

4 Study photos **A–H**.
a Think of three words to describe each image.
b For each image, say whether it is showing sustainable or unsustainable development.

OVER TO YOU

c Write a sentence to explain your choice in each case.
d Draw an opinion line like the one below. Along your line write the letters of the photos, arranging them according to their level of sustainability or unsustainability.

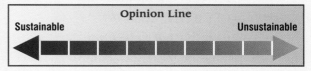

Opinion Line

Sustainable   Unsustainable

e Write a paragraph to explain why you have chosen the projects at each end of your opinion line.

5 Use the images that you have identified as sustainable to make a video storyboard. You need to write a voice-over to be narrated, explaining what sustainable development is. You could use copies of the images to create a PowerPoint presentation, entering your narration text for each slide in outline view.

In this unit you have learned about:

- different definitions of development
- world poverty, its causes and why it is unevenly spread
- ways of using data to measure and analyse development patterns
- what governments, voluntary groups and individuals can do to support development
- the importance of sustainable development, and fair trade.

Some 82% of Niger's population relies on subsistence farming and cattle rearing. They try to grow enough food to feed themselves from harvest to harvest. The United Nations estimates that 2.5 million of Niger's 12 million people live on less than one meal per day, and survive on wild roots and leaves. Before the current crisis shown in news article **A**, 40% of children were malnourished. Niger has one of the lowest literacy rates in the world.

Fantastic Facts

- Over the past 40 years, life expectancy at birth in LEDCs has increased by 20 years – about as much as was achieved in all of human history before the middle of the 20th century.
- Over the past 30 years, adult illiteracy in the developing world has been cut nearly in half, from 47 to 25%.
- Over the past 20 years, the number of people living on less than $1 a day has fallen by 200 million.

Niger's people living on the edge

A

July–August 2005

The United Nations reckons that 3.6 million people in Niger will go hungry before the next harvest begins in October. It's a silent tsunami, says World Vision.

Families are feeding their children grass and leaves from the trees to keep them alive. Most of the famine victims have no money left and many have sold their farm implements, their livestock and even their jewellery to raise cash to buy food in a market that is becoming increasingly expensive

Children who have wasted away to little more than skin and bones lie on the floor, while other children are forced to drink the medicated porridge and milk

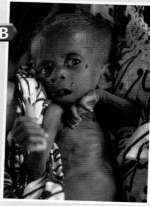
B

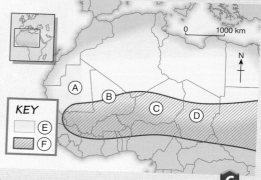
C

Almost 8 million people are at risk of hunger in the entire Sahel region of West Africa, one of the most neglected and poorest regions in the world

KEY

E

F

D

A tonne of locusts, which is a tiny part of the average swarm, eats the same amount of food in a single day as 10 elephants, 25 camels or 2500 people

Since August 2004, the rains have failed. Crops and grazing land were also devastated by swarms of locusts, the biggest invasion for 20 years. In this harsh environment, people cope by selling animals, men move away to work, and nomads move their animals towards available pasture.

The Niger crisis of 2005 had been predicted since October 2003. Locust invasions could have been checked by spraying the locust populations early. When the first appeal for aid was made, it would have cost only $1 per day, per person to prevent malnutrition among children. Now that the situation has worsened and people are weaker, it will cost $80 to save a malnourished child's life. It took images of dying children to 'make the world wake up'.

These images of Niger represent the extreme edge of world poverty. They can distort perceptions about the reality of life in most LEDCs. They also run the risk of making us who live in MEDCs think there's no point in responding to the need because it is too great.

OVER TO YOU

1 Look at map **C**. Name the following:
- countries A–D (the countries most under threat)
- physical regions E and F.

2 **a** Read news article **A** carefully and try to identify the causes of the disaster in Niger.
  b Discuss each cause with a partner. Try to decide whether it is a long-term or short-term cause.
  c Draw a two-column table and summarise the causes. Use one column for long-term causes and the other for short-term causes.
  d Decide how important each cause is. Lightly shade the boxes on your table as follows:
  - very important causes – *red*
  - important causes – *orange*
  - less important causes – *yellow*.

3 **a** Draw a development compass rose (DCR) in the centre of a large sheet of paper.
  b Write two questions for each point on your DCR, about the Niger crisis.
  c Work with a partner. First compare your questions and then write a description for each point on the DCR, answering your key questions.

4 **a** Go back to map **A** on pages 26–27. Find Niger and its three neighbouring countries under threat in the crisis.
  b What is the GDP band for each country?
  c Now turn to pages 28–29 and record the Human Development Index for each of the four countries.
  d Look back at the World Bank GIS website shown on pages 30–31. Use the internet to collect further data for the four countries.
  e Summarise your findings in a table.
  f Write a paragraph summing up what this data tells you about the level of development in these four countries.

5 **a** Go back to pages 32–33. Make links between what you have discovered about Niger and its neighbours, and the causes of world poverty.
  b Identify the three most relevant causes in the region. Explain your choices.

6 Look back at the Millennium Development Goals on page 34. Which goals are most important to the Sahel region?

7 Read the extracts below and then the 'Fantastic Facts'.

  a Your class may have a debate about the impact of media coverage on the Niger aid disaster.

  Is public opinion about developing countries distorted in the UK by media coverage?

  > My major concern about the way LEDC issues and countries are portrayed in the European media is that most often our people appear as victims – of hunger, disease, poverty, corruption. There is little effort made to portray the people as active participants and subjects in their society, despite their poor conditions.

  Luis Hernandez, Centro de Estudios para el Cambio en el Campo Mexicano, Mexico City

  A recent survey found that **80%** of the British public believe that the developing world exists in a permanent state of disaster.

  b Write a report on the effects of media coverage on the Niger famine.

3 Comparing Countries

A continent divided?

Where are we going?

In this unit you will learn to:

- **ask geographical questions about Mexico and the USA**
- **develop a sequence for investigation**
- **select relevant information in order to aid comparison of two countries**
- **present data effectively to highlight similarities and differences**
- **consider the interdependence of nations.**

Look at front cover resource **B**, which is a map of North and South America, and see if you can locate Mexico and the USA.

All of the images on these two pages come from Mexico and the United States of America (USA). These two countries are both part of the vast North American continent and they share a common border that is over 2500 km long. They display some similarities in landscape, climate and culture, yet they are distinctly different in many important ways. They have a shared and at times turbulent history, and their relations with each other have changed through time.

Mexico and the USA also have a surprising variety of links with the UK, which helps us understand a little about both countries. But how well do we really know Mexico or the USA? Is our knowledge reliable, or is it the product of stereotypical images from TV and film?

E

F

The skills you develop through this unit will enable you to go on to research any country by:

- asking relevant questions
- producing well-organised reports with supporting evidence
- using ICT to find out the important information and transform your data into powerful presentations.

These skills are required in most modern jobs, which is why geographers are in demand in many businesses. The jobs of the future will not depend on what you know, but on *how you learn*.

OVER TO YOU

1. Which of the photos **A–F** could have come from Mexico or the USA only, and which could have been taken in either country?

2. Use a Venn diagram to show how you have assigned them to 'USA', 'Mexico' or 'Both'. Give reasons for your choices.

3. Why is it difficult to say where some images may have come from?

4. **a** Write down 10 words you would most associate with each country (20 in total).

    b Compare your words with your partner's. From your combined answers, decide on the most important 5 for each country. Give reasons for your choices.

5. From your work on the photos and words related to these two countries, write a paragraph to explain how they show there are some similarities and some differences in the way we view Mexico and the USA.

    Hint: This is your first effort – we will come back to these perceptions later.

In this unit you will consider how to study a large topic (Mexico and the USA are big places!) and select the key aspects you believe are essential to compare and contrast these two places. Looking for similarities and differences, and then explaining why both occur, is a core skill in geography. You will investigate the geography of Mexico and the USA and produce an extended piece of work. Some important areas to be considered are contained within this unit. You will want to develop these further and add other areas of study that are of interest to you. This means thinking about the big questions that need to be asked rather than the small issues that don't really tell us a great deal about these two great nations.

Horizons 1 Unit 2 'People' and this book Unit 2 '80:20'.

What do we need to know about these places?

**Together, Mexico and the USA have a total area of 11 760 000 km²
and a combined population of 400 million people. Consider how
varied those areas are and how diverse the millions of people
are in their location, culture and work.**

The most important part of your work in comparing them is to decide on
which aspects must be included in your final report. By asking the important
questions in a suitable order, you can ensure a logical flow to the comparison
and avoid including irrelevant or poorly organised information.

C *Describing where people live is
useful, but explaining why they
live there tells us more.*

Remember what you
have learned so far **A**

A The introduction must
set the scene by telling
us which
countries
are being
compared
and why.

B *I think you need to know
something about the
location, size and physical
features of a place before
finding out about the people
who live on this land.*

D *A good answer quotes
facts and figures to
support the argument.
For example, '...300 die in
the Sonoran Desert...'*

E *It's easier to understand
graphs than raw data, but the
graphs must be clear and have
the right titles and labels.*

F *Pictures, maps and graphs
are better than long
descriptions, but are only
really helpful if they are
supported by comments
related to the task.*

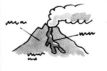

G *The final conclusion is really
important because it is where you
make up your mind about something.
It should be a decision, opinion or
judgement reached after
consideration. It's where you decide
what your
answer is and
what it might
mean for the
countries
described.*

Conclusion

How much money does each person share from the national wealth?

What is the total area?

What jobs do people do?

When does the climate present problems for people?

Where are Mexico and the USA?

Where do most people live?

Why do few people choose to live in some areas?

Who controls the country?

Help!

Imagine the finished product.

Extended writing, reports and projects rarely suffer because they are too short. We don't tend to put too little in but too much! Using an advanced organiser helps us organise our time, set criteria for success and gives us times to check our work. This is made even easier if we can imagine what a finished, successful report will contain – and what it won't. Try listing what your report should include, and let those aims guide you.

B Which questions do you need to ask first?

C
- 'The USA is more developed than Mexico because of its resources.'
- 'Mexico will rival the USA by the end of the 21st century.'
- 'The gap between the USA and Mexico will grow ever wider.'

OVER TO YOU

1 Think of 10 questions you need to find answers to during this investigation.

2 Share your answers with your partner and decide on the best 10 from the possible 20 available.

3 Try to arrange these into a logical order – which will you need to find out about first? (*Hint:* Some ideas from diagram **B** might help you.) These questions can help you organise your enquiry.

4 Choose a title for your report. It could be very simple, for example: 'A comparison of Mexico and the USA.'

Alternatively, the title could be a hypothesis to be proved or disproved. This can give a focus to your investigations and is especially useful because it helps you come to a conclusion. From the selection in box **C**, or from your own discussions, choose a title for your report.

5 Devise an advanced organiser to help you plan your project – your teacher may provide you with one.

In *Horizons 1* you looked at where people live and why population is more dense in some places than in others.

Population density varies for both physical and human reasons. Some places are easier to inhabit than others because they have a more suitable topography, altitude, climate, soil and access to fresh water. Physical factors affect how easy it is to live in a region. Negative zones are characterised by extremes of these factors. Human factors, including historical and political influences, can also have major effects on where people live. For example, border settlements such as Cuidad Juarez may grow even though they have few physical advantages. Economic reasons help to explain the growth of oil towns such as Dallas.

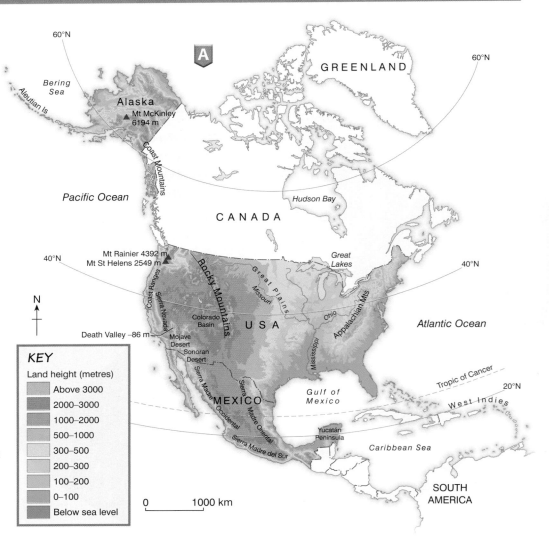

A

KEY
Land height (metres)
- Above 3000
- 2000–3000
- 1000–2000
- 500–1000
- 300–500
- 200–300
- 100–200
- 0–100
- Below sea level

0   1000 km

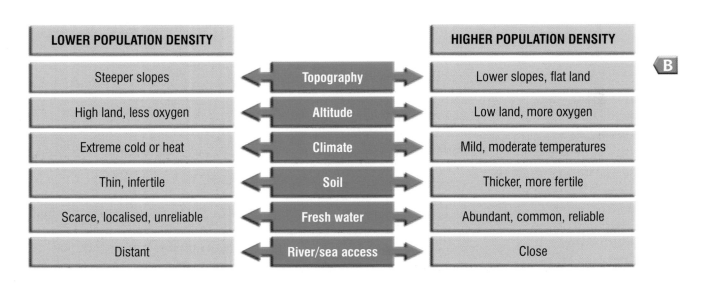

B

LOWER POPULATION DENSITY		HIGHER POPULATION DENSITY
Steeper slopes	Topography	Lower slopes, flat land
High land, less oxygen	Altitude	Low land, more oxygen
Extreme cold or heat	Climate	Mild, moderate temperatures
Thin, infertile	Soil	Thicker, more fertile
Scarce, localised, unreliable	Fresh water	Abundant, common, reliable
Distant	River/sea access	Close

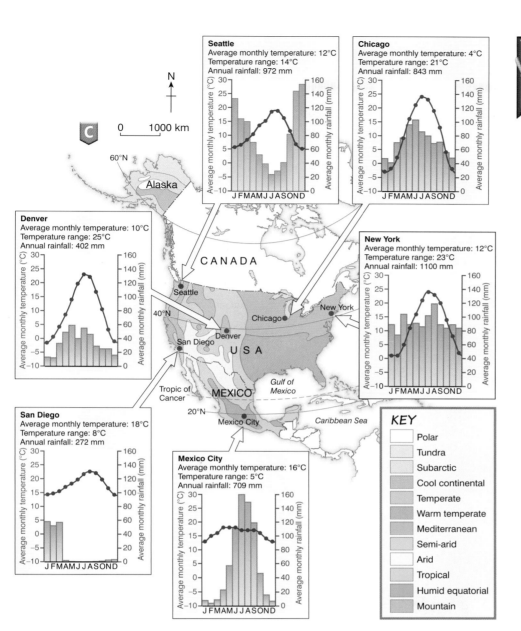

Seattle
Average monthly temperature: 12°C
Temperature range: 14°C
Annual rainfall: 972 mm

Chicago
Average monthly temperature: 4°C
Temperature range: 21°C
Annual rainfall: 843 mm

Denver
Average monthly temperature: 10°C
Temperature range: 25°C
Annual rainfall: 402 mm

New York
Average monthly temperature: 12°C
Temperature range: 23°C
Annual rainfall: 1100 mm

San Diego
Average monthly temperature: 18°C
Temperature range: 8°C
Annual rainfall: 272 mm

Mexico City
Average monthly temperature: 16°C
Temperature range: 5°C
Annual rainfall: 709 mm

KEY
- Polar
- Tundra
- Subarctic
- Cool continental
- Temperate
- Warm temperate
- Mediterranean
- Semi-arid
- Arid
- Tropical
- Humid equatorial
- Mountain

Help!

A description that identifies extreme differences or obvious similarities is a good start.
If facts, figures and place names (evidence) are added, it will make it a stronger answer.
A description with evidence that compares and contrasts different places in one country or in other countries is better still.

The maps on these pages show some aspects of the physical nature of these two countries. But you will need more information gathered from your research to complete the picture. What other physical features from the list below would be most useful in comparing Mexico and the USA?

- Soil quality maps
- Length of growing season
- Temperature in January and July
- Hours of sunshine
- Volcanoes and earthquakes
- Tropical storms and floods.

OVER TO YOU

1 For each country, describe the topography (see map **A** and front cover resource **B**).
Mention the following factors:
a the physical extent of the country (north to south, east to west)
b the amount of upland and lowland
c the number and extent of major rivers.

2 For each country, describe the variations in climate (map **C**). Find at least two similarities and differences. Suggest reasons for these differences.

3 Using diagram **B**, suggest what effects these variations might have on:
a total population in each country
b where people are likely and unlikely to live.

4 Decide which other aspects – physical, climatic, environmental – of these two countries you wish to explore further.

Hint: Some are listed in the bullet points above, and you can find more information on the weblink.

WEBLINKS You will find a link to the US Geological Survey website at
www.nelsonthornes.com/horizons

Are the populations alike?

When you compare the peoples of two nations, it is easy to find data telling you where they live and how many they are. But it is important to sift through the information to find the important facts that help you compare them effectively.

For example, Mexico and the USA share some astonishing population statistics. The USA is estimated to have a population of 297 million, making it the 3rd biggest country in the world, whereas the population of Mexico is 105 million, making it 11th in the world. These figures should trigger some searching questions:

- Does that mean they are **overpopulated**? (Can they support this many people?)
- Which is growing the faster? (What kinds of problems do fast-growing countries face?)
- Are the people evenly spread? (Why do some areas attract high densities of people?)

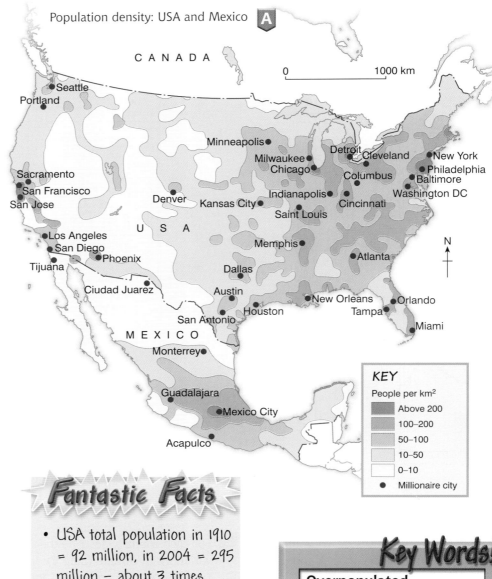

Population density: USA and Mexico **A**

KEY
People per km²
- Above 200
- 100–200
- 50–100
- 10–50
- 0–10
- ● Millionaire city

Fantastic Facts

- USA total population in 1910 = 92 million, in 2004 = 295 million – about 3 times greater.
- Mexico total population in 1910 = 15 million, in 2004 = 105 million – 7 times greater.

Key Words!

Overpopulated

Places where the total population cannot be supported by a country's resources (raw materials, money, industrial facilities, labour).

B Changes in total population

	1900	1930	1960	1990	1995	2000	2005
Mexico	13 607 259	16 552 722	30 000 000	81 249 645	91 158 290	97 483 412	105 000 000
USA	76 094 000	123 076 741	180 671 158	249 438 712	262 764 948	281 421 906	297 753 096

An analysis of maps **A** and **C** on pages 48–49 will help you answer the last question. There are some strong correlations (relationships) between the more positive environments and higher concentrations of population in both countries. Try to name some places that are good examples of the general pattern, but also identify anomalies (changes from the normal pattern). For example, Mexico City seems to suffer from high altitude and appears to be too far from a major river or the sea.

These countries developed at different times (table **B**) and with different influences. Their ethnic diversity (diagrams **C** and **D**) tells us a lot about the past of their peoples and suggests how they might change in the future.

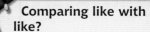

Comparing like with like?
Countries do not classify or measure data in the same way. Ethnic group in the USA is based on a person's own answer in the census ('you are what you say you are'). Hispanics are not identified as a separate group but can be of any race.
In Mexico, ethnic group is identified mainly by the language spoken.

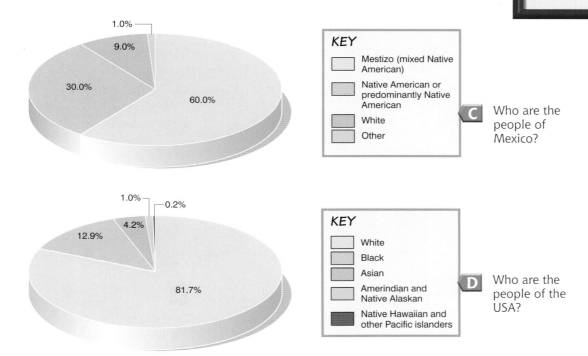

KEY
- Mestizo (mixed Native American)
- Native American or predominantly Native American
- White
- Other

C Who are the people of Mexico?

KEY
- White
- Black
- Asian
- Amerindian and Native Alaskan
- Native Hawaiian and other Pacific islanders

D Who are the people of the USA?

1 Describe the pattern of population distribution in each country.

Hint: Use terms such as *north-south-east, north-south-west, central* and *coastal*.

2 Using your findings from the previous pages, suggest at least three reasons for the ways population density varies across both countries.

Hint: Consider altitude, rivers, coast and climate.

3 Are there any similarities between both countries in terms of:
a population density
b the reasons for variation in population density?

4 a Use the figures in table **B** to draw a total population line graph showing how both countries have changed over time.
b Add a title and labels to your graph, and pinpoint at least two times when you think population changed significantly in either country.
c Annotate your graph to explain why you think these changes are significant.

5 Study graphs **C** and **D**. Describe the differences between the two countries. Suggest explanations for the variations.

OVER TO YOU

WEBLINKS You will find links to the US census and Mexican government websites at www.nelsonthornes.com/horizons

What do they do?

Economic factors affect what a country produces and the wealth it generates. They influence how many people a country can support and their quality of life.

Map **A** shows how the land is used for agriculture and industry in these two countries. The USA has far more agricultural land than Mexico but has a lower percentage of agricultural workers than Mexico (graphs **B** and **C**). Advanced farming techniques allow the USA to be the biggest exporter of grain in the world and the second biggest meat producer.

Although nearly half of Mexico's total land area is classified as agricultural, only 12% of the total area is cultivated, and 80% of the cultivated land requires regular irrigation. Agricultural practices range from traditional **slash-and-burn cultivation** for family subsistence, to capital-intensive export agriculture.

Graphs **B** and **C** show some information about the types of jobs in Mexico and the USA. These may be used as indicators of how developed each country is (graph **D**).

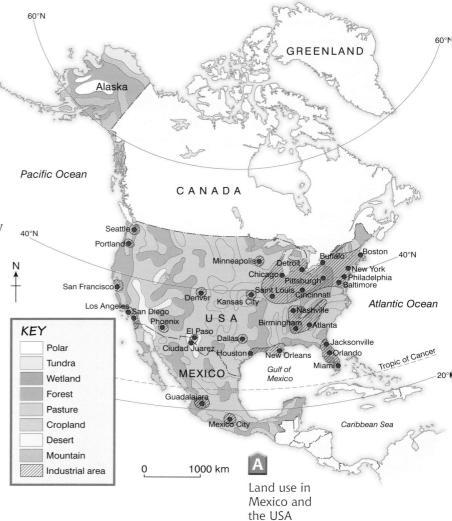

KEY

	Polar
	Tundra
	Wetland
	Forest
	Pasture
	Cropland
	Desert
	Mountain
	Industrial area

0   1000 km

A

Land use in Mexico and the USA

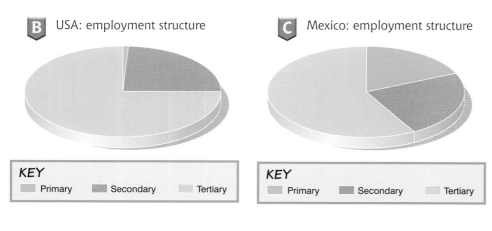

B USA: employment structure

KEY
Primary   Secondary   Tertiary

C Mexico: employment structure

KEY
Primary   Secondary   Tertiary

Key Words!

LEDCs

Less economically developed countries.

MEDCs

More economically developed countries.

Underemployed

People who are underemployed usually work in the informal sector – that is, work that is not regular or recognised officially by the government. It is often very low-paid work.

 **Links to...**

In your work on development in *Horizons 1* Unit 5 'Work', you were introduced to the idea that countries can be classified according to the structure of their industry (percentage of primary, secondary and tertiary industries).

LEDCs tend to have more workers in primary industries, and fewer tertiary industries.
MEDCs have shed many jobs in these areas and show higher levels of tertiary industry.

Economic factors are only part of the story, and a variety of indicators is needed to determine the level of development in any country (table **E**).

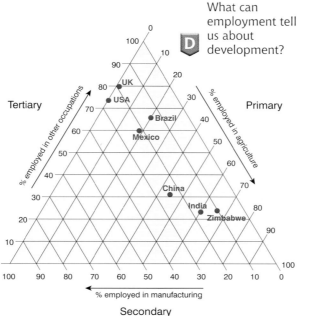

What can employment tell us about development?

D

Tertiary

Primary

Secondary

% employed in other occupations

% employed in agriculture

% employed in manufacturing

Help!

Graph **D** is an **appropriate** style of graph – it shows three variables (three types of industry) so it has three axes. It is also **effective** because it shows more clearly than a table of figures how these variables may be used to classify countries. The labelled axes and interpretive comments make the graph easy to understand, and help the reader to make comparisons. **Transforming** data like this is an important skill in coursework at Key Stages 4 and 5.

Fantastic Facts

- The median age for Mexico is 24.9 years, USA 36.7 years.
- The workforce in Mexico = 34.7 million, 3.5% unemployed, up to 25% **underemployed**.
- The workforce in USA = 147.4 million, including 5.5% unemployed.

E Is there a link between the economy and quality of life?

Indicator	Mexico	USA
Population growth rate (%)	1.17	0.92
Birth rate (births/1000 people)	21.01	14.14
Death rate (deaths/1000 people)	4.73	8.25
Migrants (per 1000 people)	–4.57	3.31
Infant mortality rate (deaths/1000 live births)	20.91	6.50
Life expectancy (years)	75.19	77.71
Literacy (%)	92.2	97.0
GDP (trillion US $)	1.006	11.750
GDP per capita (US $)	9600	40 100
Human Development Index (HDI) value (world rank)	0.802 (53)	0.939 (8)
Doctors per 100 000 people	156	279

OVER TO YOU

1 Describe the pattern of land use shown in map **A**. In particular, try to describe the location and estimate the approximate percentages for the area involved in:
  a agriculture (especially cropland)
  b industry.

2 Using your findings from the previous pages, suggest why agriculture varies:
  a within each country
  b between the two countries.

3 Study graphs **B** and **C** and describe the patterns of employment shown. How do these graphs relate to your description of land use in map **A** (activity 1)? For example, do the countries with the largest areas devoted to agriculture have a significant primary sector?

4 How does graph **D** help to identify similarities between the USA and Mexico in terms of development?

5 The development indicators in table **E** show us other methods of assessing what a country is like for the people who live there, or who deal with it. Select the three most important factors from your point of view and explain how they show similarities or differences between the two countries.

Are there differences within each country?

Comparisons can be made at any scale. So far you have concentrated on comparing key features of two countries. You can add depth to your study by looking at the differences that exist within one country. In this example we are going to compare two regions within the USA.

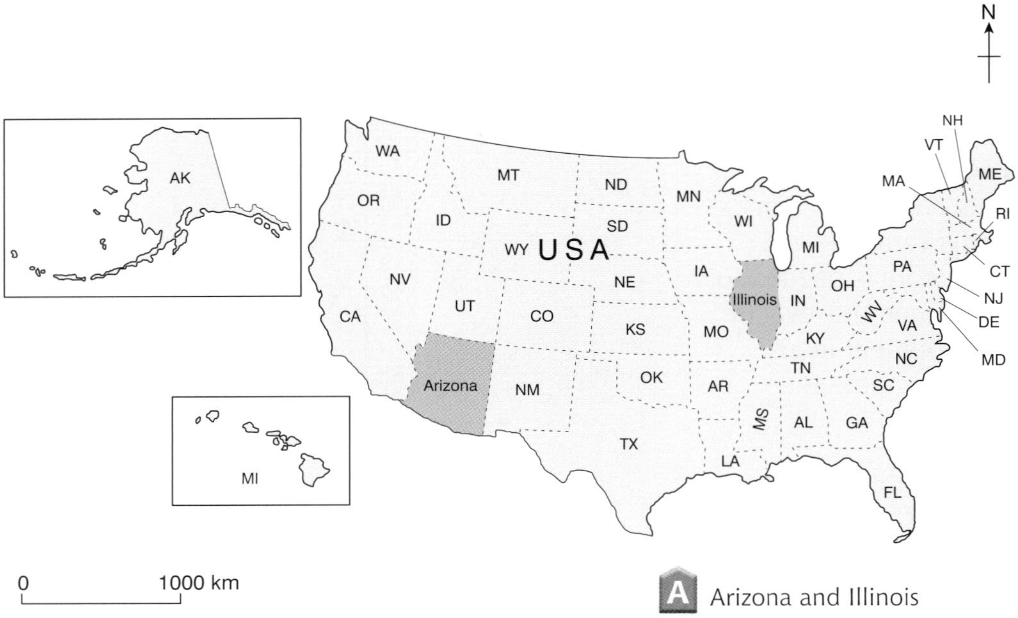

A   Arizona and Illinois

0   1000 km

The desert lands of Arizona reflect its low precipitation levels. Water storage and irrigation are crucial to farming here. When it joined the USA in 1912, Arizona was the biggest cotton producer in America and cattle ranching occupied a lot of the land. Later these were over taken by the copper mining industry (Arizona is the USA's biggest producer, hence the copper star in the state flag). In recent years high-tech industry has been a major growth area, so the traditional advantages of 'the five Cs' – Copper, Cattle, Cotton, Citrus and Climate – have had an extra C added, for Computers.

Illinois has three major geographical divisions:

- To the north 'Chicagoland' borders Lake Michigan, and is very urban and industrialised. This flat, accessible conurbation houses over 9.5 million people and has been expanding rapidly outwards since the 1960s.

- Central Illinois is characterised by **prairie lands** where rural communities grow crops like wheat and soyabeans.

- The southern zone is warmer and supports more mixed farming as well as some coal mining and is generally more agricultural. Its industry ranges from machinery and food processing to petroleum and coal.

Use the weblink to explore Arizona and Illinois in greater depth and find out why these areas are different and what effect that has on the people who live there.

Fantastic Facts

The major cities of Phoenix in Arizona and Chicago in Illinois are 2800 km apart. If you drove that far east from London you would be close to Istanbul in Turkey!

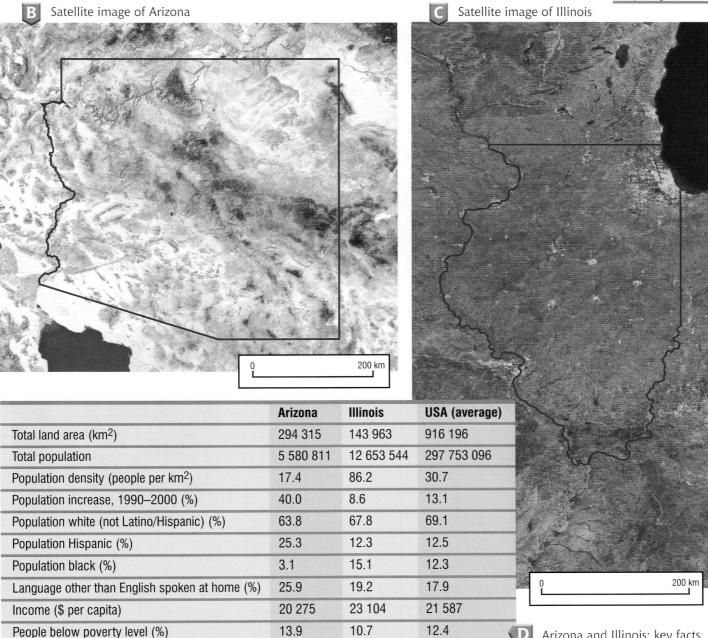

B Satellite image of Arizona

0   200 km

C Satellite image of Illinois

0   200 km

	Arizona	Illinois	USA (average)
Total land area (km²)	294 315	143 963	916 196
Total population	5 580 811	12 653 544	297 753 096
Population density (people per km²)	17.4	86.2	30.7
Population increase, 1990–2000 (%)	40.0	8.6	13.1
Population white (not Latino/Hispanic) (%)	63.8	67.8	69.1
Population Hispanic (%)	25.3	12.3	12.5
Population black (%)	3.1	15.1	12.3
Language other than English spoken at home (%)	25.9	19.2	17.9
Income ($ per capita)	20 275	23 104	21 587
People below poverty level (%)	13.9	10.7	12.4

D Arizona and Illinois: key facts

WEBLINKS   **You will find links to learn more about Arizona and Illinois at**
www.nelsonthornes.com/horizons

OVER TO YOU

1 Using distances and directions, describe the location of Arizona and Illinois within the USA (map **A**).

2 Referring to satellite images **B** and **C**, comment on any differences you see between the two states.

3 How does the information in table **D** suggest the two states are different? Choose three key statistics, e.g. related to land use, population or wealth, to provide data supporting your comments.

4 Select *either* Arizona *or* Illinois. Imagine you are on a twinning committee trying to explain why people from the other state should want to be twinned with your state.

Prepare a five-minute presentation with a script to explain the differences and in particular the interesting points about your state.

5 Use an internet search to conduct a similar comparison between two Mexican states.

How are Mexico and the USA connected?

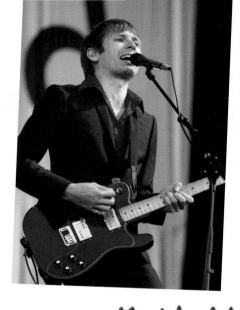

A Cars and guitars are American icons – but do they know where many of their products are really made?

From being colonised by European powers in the 16th century to being major *trading partners* today, Mexico and the USA have many links (timeline *B*). People are one of the biggest links: 13.3% of the population of the USA are Hispanic in origin, including 10 million Mexicans and a total of 16 million citizens of Mexican origin (map *C*).

Many Mexicans living legally or illegally in the USA send money back to their families in Mexico. This helps the home economy as more goods and services are then bought in Mexico. In the USA, especially in some south-western states, the Mexican workforce does many of the jobs most Americans won't do because working conditions and rates of pay are so poor. Without Mexican labour, the economy of some states would be near collapse.

In fact, the Mexican economy remains closely linked to that of the USA (table **E**). For example, the Mexican *maquiladoras*, which are largely based in northern Mexico, rely almost entirely on the US market. The USA accounts for 88% of Mexican exports and provides 56% of its imports.

Key Words!

Maquiladoras

Mexican assembly plants for manufactured goods of all sorts.

USA

1775 American Revolution: Declaration of Independence 1776.

1846–48 US/Mexican war. Mexico gave up modern-day California, Arizona, New Mexico, Texas and parts of Colorado, Nevada and Utah – nearly 50% of its land.

1860–65 American Civil War: southern Confederate pro-slavery states against abolitionist northern states. Confederates defeated.

1914 and 1916 American troops intervene in Mexico.

1953–54 3.8 million Mexicans, legal and illegal, deported from USA.

B What will the timeline show in 50 years?

| 1780 | 1800 | 1820 | 1840 | 1860 | 1880 | 1900 | 1920 | 1940 | 1960 | 1980 | 2000 | 2005 |

1821 Mexico gains independence from Spain.

1853 Mexico loses area around Tucson. Last change to border.

1910 Mexican Revolution begins.

1976 Huge oil reserves discovered in southern state of Chiapas.

1994 NAFTA, USA, Canada and Mexico cooperate in trade. Big boost in border populations.

Mexico

Many of the *maquiladoras* supply parts to major firms such as General Motors (GM) in Mexico (resources **A** and **D**). This giant American-owned transnational corporation has assembly lines producing 'American' cars such as Pontiacs, Chevrolets and Chryslers for markets in the USA and the rest of the world. Since it began there in 1935, GM Mexico has grown to be the country's single largest private employer, and in return it has access to skilled, low-cost labour, which boosts profits. The Fender guitar plant at Ensenada, Mexico, began in 1987. Today, Fender Mexico builds prestigious vintage telecasters which are sold in the USA.

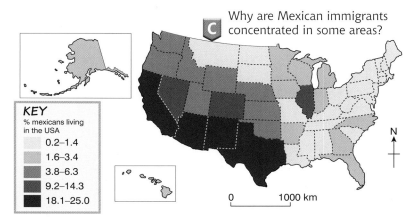

C Why are Mexican immigrants concentrated in some areas?

KEY
% mexicans living in the USA
- 0.2–1.4
- 1.6–3.4
- 3.8–6.3
- 9.2–14.3
- 18.1–25.0

0   1000 km

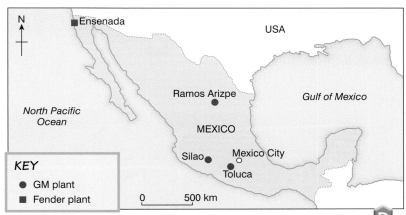

KEY
- ● GM plant
- ■ Fender plant

0   500 km

D Major US companies such as GM vehicles and Fender guitars locate factories in Mexico to benefit from lower production costs

Top 10 imports to USA from Mexico	Value in US$
1 Manufactured parts and accessories	19 306 245
2 Crude oil	17 966 592
3 Passenger cars new and used	11 171 474
4 Television receivers, VCRs other video equipment	8 966 677
5 Complete and assembled parts	8 176 023
6 Electrical apparatus and parts	6 741 325
7 Telecommunications equipment	5 327 015
8 Computers	4 610 872
9 Clothing and household goods (cotton)	4 440 149
10 Engines and engine parts	4 319 881
Total imports to USA from Mexico	***155 901 521***

Top 10 exports from USA to Mexico	Value in US$
1 Electrical apparatus	8 450 366
2 Manufactured parts and accessories of vehicles	8 224 213
3 Computer accessories	7 120 095
4 Semiconductors	5 448 367
5 Plastic materials	5 000 361
6 Other industrial supplies	3 457 680
7 Assorted minor goods/shipments	3 347 992
8 Finished metal shapes	3 219 767
9 Industrial machines	3 145 322
10 Telecommunications equipment	3 138 182
Total exports from USA to Mexico	***110 834 985***

E Selected US/Mexican imports and exports

1. Which of the items in photos **A** are sometimes made in Mexico for the USA?

2. Identify at least one way in which timeline **B** reflects links between the USA and Mexico based on:
   - **a** land
   - **b** war
   - **c** population
   - **d** trade.

3. Describe and suggest reasons for the distributions of Mexicans living in the USA.

4. What are the most important products traded between the countries?

5. Are their any differences in the nature of the products, e.g. primary products and basic foods or manufactured goods?

6. Extend your study of links between the two countries by looking at some related issues, such as:
   - free trade organisations (GATT and NAFTA)
   - other imports and exports (e.g. financial services)
   - air routes
   - cultural exchanges
   - Americans living in Mexico (e.g. second homes)
   - holiday exchange travel
   - cross-border cooperation.

How are these countries linked to the UK?

As the USA was once a colony of Great Britain, 19% of Americans can trace their ancestry back to the UK. With their shared language, culture and history, the USA and UK became close allies in war and peace. Mexico developed economically far later than the USA. Its largely Spanish-speaking culture and relatively minor role as a world power meant there were fewer links with Britain. Today these three countries are linked more closely than might be thought at first.

The figures in table **F** show just how much the trading links with each country and the UK are worth. Both countries have a net trade deficit with the UK, so Britain currently has a trade surplus with them. In the case of Mexico (graphs **C** and **D**), we import raw materials such as petroleum products but our main imports are manufactured goods. Services like tourism are also important and Britons make up an increasing proportion of the 20 million or so people who visit Mexico annually, and help to make tourism Mexico's third biggest earner.

However, trade figures alone do not always tell the whole story. Our links with each other have cultural and social dimensions as well. The photos in **A** and **B** show some of the links, but how many more can you name? It's hard to imagine popular music in Britain without the American inspirations of jazz, rock and roll and hip-hop. American film and TV have a huge influence on culture in the UK. The influence of Mexico in the UK might not seem so great but from Latino music to Mexican food there are increasing signs that we are more interested in what Mexico has to offer (photos **B** and article **E**).

A

B

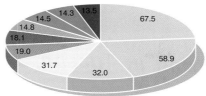

C UK imports from Mexico, 2004 (£ millions)

67.5
58.9
32.0
31.7
19.0
18.1
14.8
14.5
14.3
13.5

KEY

- ☐ Telecoms and sound recording equipment
- ☐ Office machines and equipment
- ☐ Petroleum and petroleum products
- ☐ Power-generating equipment
- ☐ Other transport equipment
- ■ Miscellaneous manufactured articles
- ☐ Electrical machinery
- ☐ General industrial machinery
- ■ Plastics in primary forms
- ■ Non-ferrous metals

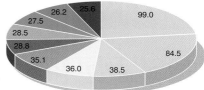

D UK exports to Mexico, 2004 (£ millions)

99.0
84.5
38.5
36.0
35.1
28.8
28.5
27.5
26.2
25.6

KEY

- ☐ Road vehicles
- ☐ Medicinal and pharmaceutical products
- ☐ Electrical machinery
- ☐ Chemical materials and products
- ■ Specialised industrial machinery
- ■ Power-generating equipment
- ☐ Essential oils and resinoids
- ■ Beverages
- ■ Organic chemicals
- ■ General industrial machinery

E

Ay caramba! Mexican Food on Target to Outsell Chinese

By Louise Barnett, Independent Online, 4 June 2005

Forget the chow mein and pass the enchiladas. Familiar Chinese food is falling out of favour with Britons who are attracted by spicy Mexican fare. Purchases of Latino items such as tortillas, refried beans, fajitas and quesadillas were up 10 per cent in the past year, the market analysts TNS said. If the current trend continues, Mexican will have overtaken Chinese to become the UK's second favourite ethnic cuisine in 2007. James Beaton, founder of the Mexican grocery brand Discovery Foods, said: 'Indian and Chinese have been huge favourites with Brits for many years, so perhaps it's not surprising that people are now starting to look elsewhere for a spicy, ethnic fix.'

Country	Exports to the UK (US$ million)	Position	Imports from the UK (US$ million)	Position
USA	36 000	4th	46 400	6th
Mexico	733	7th	1 242	12th

F Trade with the UK, 2004

Fantastic Facts

British Airways flies to 57 airports in the USA and 2 in Mexico.

OVER TO YOU

1 a Which country has the most valuable trading links with the UK, Mexico or the USA?
 b Suggest why this might be.
 c Does it have a trade surplus or deficit?

2 a Study graphs **C** and **D**. Describe the differences between the goods the UK trades with Mexico.

 b Which of our Mexican imports surprises you most? Explain why.

3 Do you think there are other links between our countries that are less easily measured? Try to name three things that don't feature in the trade figures but may be important connections between the UK, Mexico and the USA.

4 Find out what products the UK trades with the USA. Are they similar to or different from those traded between the UK and Mexico?

Mystery

Why is John Doe staying in Tucson, Arizona?

Assessment task

In comparing and contrasting Mexico and the USA during this unit, it is clear they not only have a shared history but also a shared destiny. By studying a topical issue such as illegal immigration, which affects both countries, it is possible to illustrate some of the wider issues that affect both countries. The mystery of 'John Doe' is one of a thousand true stories that raises many questions about each country.

Discussion point

Read the statements in resource **C**. These could have been written about North Africa and Europe, or a host of other places worldwide. Problems of economic migration are likely to accelerate all over the world. Who is responsible?

- Is it the countries losing population because they have failed to develop and provide for their people?

- Is it the richer countries because they have failed to help the poorer ones make conditions there more conducive to staying put?

- Is it individuals because they seek to do the best for themselves and not for the country they are leaving or entering?

Think before you speak! What would you *really* do if *you* couldn't get work, had no support, and had a family to feed?

Chris Simcox, leader of the Minutemen patriots (vigilantes), at the border fence in Arizona

B

A Migrants are stopped at the border

C Mystery statements

A Jobs in some areas of Mexico are declining as transnational firms switch production to China.	**B** Governor of California Arnold Schwarzenegger says he thinks the Minutemen are 'doing a great job'.	**C** A Samaritan from a Christian group 'No More Deaths' found John and tried to revive him with water.	**D** The severe measures necessary to 'seal the border' are unlikely to be acceptable to the American voters.
E Border patrol guards looking for drug dealers opened fire on a man who ran when challenged.	**F** When he was picked up he muttered a friend's name and repeated the word 'Tucson'.	**G** John Doe is a name given to any unidentified person in the USA.	**H** The temperature hit 41°C for at least 5 days in the desert that week.
I A Mexican woman and a child of 5 were found dead in the same desert area the next day. 300 died there in 2004.	**J** Minutemen are vigilantes who go armed into the desert of Arizona and California to find 'illegals'.	**K** The American Border Action Group aims to help the 'illegals' get to safety.	**L** Arizona is seen as the easiest place to cross the border now that California and Texas have tightened security.
M John cannot remember his name. He carried a mobile phone bought in Pueblo, Mexico.	**N** The Mexican government has produced a comic-book-style guide to staying alive in the desert for migrants.	**O** The ambassador says that the wealth of the USA will always 'pull' and Mexican poverty will always 'push' migrants.	**P** A border crossing guide costs about $1500, including rooms and transport.
Q With coffee selling at only 60 cents a pound, many Mexican farmers have sold up.	**R** The Border Action Group keeps water tanks in the desert to help dehydrated people.	**S** The Sonora Desert in Arizona is 80 km wide and has high mountains (2000+ metres) which have to be crossed.	**T** Illegal immigrants are deported back to Mexico when they are found by the border patrol guards.
U 500 000 'illegals' were arrested in the Tucson sector in 2004.	**V** A Minutemen patriot thought he 'spooked' someone like John Doe in the Sonora Desert.	**W** Doctors at Tucson hospital say heat exhaustion and dehydration can lead to permanent brain damage.	**X** In 2004, Mexicans abroad sent back $16.6 bn (£8.9 bn), making it the second largest source of income for Mexico after oil.

OVER TO YOU

1 Use the statements in resource **C** to work out why John Doe is staying in Tucson. There is no one true answer and it may be a combination of factors. Your teacher may provide the cards to sort into groups.

2 Try to sort them into 3 to 5 categories according to the similarities and links you see between the evidence on the cards.

Remember: When you have worked out why you think he is staying in Tucson, Arizona, you will have to justify your story by explaining how the facts support your argument. The more facts you can use, the stronger your answer will be. If you think some facts are less important, be prepared to say why.

3 Write your answer in less than 500 words.

Comparing Countries

How has my opinion changed?

Your first task in this unit asked you to assign a series of pictures either to Mexico or to the USA. They were chosen to expose some of the stereotypes we hold about those countries. As you have learned more, some of your perceptions will have changed. The similarities and differences you saw initially may not be the same now. Understanding how and why your views have changed is an important part of your learning.

What do I need to know now?

At the beginning of this unit you were asked to formulate a series of questions you wanted answers to. Have they been answered? Which extra questions do you need to ask now? You may need to add extra questions about things you have already researched or about totally new topics. Remember: the aim is to identify similarities and differences between these countries.

Where will these countries be in 2050?

You have spent much of your investigation describing how these countries are at the present, but both are changing fast. They will not necessarily develop in the same ways, despite their close links. From your research you will have gained an insight into the way both countries have changed in recent years. Predicting what could happen next is what planners in governments do to prepare for change before it happens. How do you think the following aspects might change by 2050? Why do people need to be aware of those changes?

A Should Mexico try to follow the American way?

- Population
- Trade and industry
- Wealth
- Environment

Satellite picture **A** shows the US–Mexican border around Mexicali (Mexico). The red colour shows where fields are irrigated to make them yield more crops. So much water was taken from the Colorado River that little was left for the Mexicans. Modern agricultural developments on the American side use far more water than is used on the south side of the border, but many question if this is sustainable. Pollution from farmland, towns and industry threaten the water quality and environment.

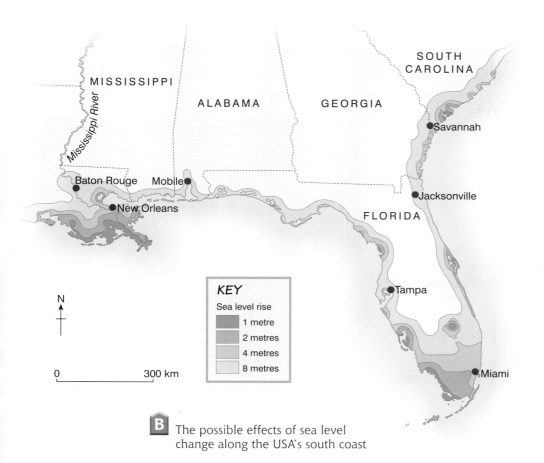

Geographers predict that sea level rise will submerge some coastal regions.

How far the coastlines will move is still being debated, but a number of cities are already under threat. Sea level rise has been linked to industrialisation and development, and increased power consumption is a major reason for higher levels of greenhouse gases.

If developing countries like Mexico follow the same route to development as the USA, global warming will get worse. What will the maps of Mexico and the USA look like then?

B The possible effects of sea level change along the USA's south coast

OVER TO YOU

In reviewing progress on your report so far, it is important to ask yourself some searching questions. This is your chance to assess how successfully you have met your initial aims.

1 What are the main differences between your views now and when you began?

2 What were the key moments/ activities that changed your mind? Explain why.

3 What questions do you need to ask now?

4 Why is it important to ask them?

5 How will these two countries be different in 2050?

6 What will have caused these changes? What might the effects be?

7 A misconception is a false impression of a real situation based on a flawed interpretation of the facts. Some of your misconceptions may have been challenged during this unit.

a All of the statements in resource **C** are wrong in some way and represent a misunderstanding of the true facts. Use the knowledge you have acquired during this unit to suggest correct interpretations.

For example: 'Mexico once owned the USA.' ➡ 'The states of New Mexico and California were controlled by Mexico until 1848.'

C

1　All of Mexico is very dry and hot.
2　The densest populations in both countries are found near the coast.
3　Mexico has no immigrants from the USA.
4　The USA has a higher density of population than Mexico.
5　Mexico is an LEDC so it produces more agricultural products than the USA.
6　Rich countries like the UK only import raw materials from Mexico.
7　Mexico has a completely different employment structure to that of the USA.

b Add at least three more misconceptions you think people might have (or that you had before you started this work). Suggest what a more appropriate interpretation might be.

4 Ecosystems

What is an ecosystem?

Where are we going?

In this unit you will learn about:

- the interactions that take place in all *ecosystems*

- the coral reef ecosystem – how it is threatened, and how it can be conserved

- the rainforest ecosystem

- the savanna grassland ecosystem and the farming systems that use it

- population and food supply in the human ecosystem.

C

D

OVER TO YOU

Look carefully at the photos on these two pages. For each photo:

1 Describe the vegetation. Refer to:
- the height of the plants
- any layers that you can see in the vegetation
- the thickness of the vegetation
- the size of leaves
- any fruit or flowers that can be seen
- the variety of plant types
etc.

2 Look for any evidence that tells you about the soil. Try to work out:
- Is the soil thick or thin?
- Is it fertile or infertile?
- What colour is it?
and so on.

3 Look for any evidence that suggests what the climate might be like. Try to find evidence for:
- temperature
- rainfall
- wind
- frost
- the seasons.

4 Look for evidence of human activities and the way they might have affected, or be affecting, that ecosystem.

5 Assess whether that ecosystem might be an interesting venue for tourists, especially ecotourists, to visit.

Remember – ecotourists travel to experience conditions in interesting ecosystems. They try to travel without damaging the environment.

What are coral ecosystems like?

The remarkable nature of ecosystems can be seen in the Gulf of Aqaba at the northern end of the Red Sea (see map *B*). Here, within a few metres of each other, you can see desert ecosystems and coral reef ecosystems. One has almost no life, and the other is teeming with a huge variety of life forms. Compare this map with front cover resource *A*. See how these rich reef ecosystems lie so close to the Sahara desert ecosystem.

On page 86 of *Horizons 2* you learned how present-day limestone rocks were formed from corals that grew 350 million years ago in the Carboniferous period. The corals that make up the limestone in Malham are fossils. There are still living corals in many parts of the world, though. They live in a specialised ecosystem.

Sunlight must pass through the water to provide energy for the ecosystem. So the water must be clear and shallow. Pollution in the water can cut out the sunlight.

Only the top layer of the coral is alive. If the living coral is damaged – by boats, souvenir hunters or divers – the whole ecosystem will be destroyed.

A coral polyp is an animal, which feeds on algae that grow in the warm water.

Fish feed in the reefs on waste from the corals, or on algae.

Small fish attract predators.

A

OVER TO YOU

1 Why are there no coral reefs:
   - off the coasts of the United Kingdom?
   - close to river estuaries where there is a lot of sediment in the water?
   - in water that is deeper than about 20 metres?
   - in areas where the sea is polluted with rubbish or chemical waste?

2 Why do the coral reefs in the Gulf of Aqaba form in lines parallel to the shore, a few metres away from the land? Why do they not form in deeper water?

3 'The sun is the source of all life on the reefs.'

   Explain what this statement means.

   Illustrate your answer by drawing a diagram of a food chain.

Fantastic Facts

Some coral reefs are over 100 million years old and are the largest living structures on Earth. The Great Barrier Reef, which is over 2000 km long, can be seen from outer space.

Temperatures must be between 25°C and 30°C.

Such warm temperatures are usually only found between 30°N and 30°S of the equator.

There must be plenty of oxygen in the water, because the corals need it to grow. So the water must be fairly rough. Waves let oxygen mix with the water.

Steady currents are needed to carry waste away from the reef.

Corals have hard parts made of calcium carbonate. A simple 'polyp' lives inside this hard shell.

Jordan is a poor country. Aqaba is its only port. There is a plan to develop Aqaba and to build:

- a new port for exporting minerals mined in Jordan, oil from Iraq, etc.
- a cruise-ship port, to bring tourists – it is hoped that many of these tourists will take trips to Petra and Wadi Rum, Jordan's two great tourist attractions, and that they will shop in Aqaba
- hotels for resident tourists – many of these will be attracted by the opportunities for diving on the reefs, while others will travel out to see the reefs from glass-bottomed boats
- the American University, for Jordanian and international students – it would have close links with universities in the USA
- a duty-free manufacturing area, where transnational companies could take advantage of cheap Jordanian labour.

B Coral reefs in the Gulf of Aqaba

4 a Name the four countries that have a coastline on the Gulf of Aqaba.
 b Find out why these countries sometimes find it difficult to work together.
 c The countries do work very closely together to reduce pollution and conserve the ecosystems in the Gulf. Explain why it is in the interests of all the countries to do this.

5 Kamel works as a diving instructor in Aqaba. He teaches snorkelling (swimming near the surface, with a tube and a face mask that allow the swimmer to breath and to see clearly underwater). He also teaches scuba diving with air tanks that allow the swimmer to go 10–20 metres below the surface. In his spare time he visits schools in the town to talk to classes about coral and to encourage young people to look after the coral.

Suggest what he might say to them about:
- the beauty and excitement of exploring coral reefs
- how conservation of the reefs could help them find jobs in future
- how careless diving and sailing can damage the whole ecosystem
- how dropping litter can pollute the water, cut out light from the reefs and kill the coral
- why it is important to conserve the coral ecosystem.

OVER TO YOU

6 Look at the list above of developments that have been planned in Aqaba.
 - How might they affect the coral reefs?
 - What might Kamel say about these developments?

Hint: He might see both good and bad points in the plans.

What are the links in an ecosystem?

Coral reefs are beautiful and delicate ecosystems. However, they are different from most of the ecosystems that we see, because they are found in the sea. Ecosystems on the land depend on the sun for their source of energy – just like coral reef ecosystems. Unlike coral reefs, though, ecosystems on land also need soil.

Ecosystems are very complex. There are many connections between different parts of the system. Changes to any part of an ecosystem can affect all the other parts. Diagram **A** shows how climate, soils, vegetation and animal life are linked together in the ecosystem.

You may have already learned quite a lot about climate. You may also know about vegetation and animal life, either from geography, or from work in science, or from your general knowledge. You probably know rather less about soil.

What makes up soil?

Soil layers or horizons **B**

Most of us don't think about soil very often. But if you do think about soil, you will realise that it is an essential part of life. Our food grows in soil. All trees, flowers and plants grow in soil. Soil is really very complex.

Look at a handful of soil. Rub it between your fingers. What are the parts that make up soil? You should notice that it contains four main parts:

- **minerals** – rock fragments that have been broken up by weathering and erosion
- **plant and animal remains** – bits of leaf, twigs and **humus** which is organic matter that has been broken down by decay
- **water** – soil usually feels damp
- **air** – there are spaces, or 'pores', between the particles of soil.

All four of these parts are essential to make soil fertile and good for growing in. In a good soil the minerals, humus and water bond together to form **crumbs**. The crumbs are separated by pores, filled with air. Water can seep down through the pores.

What are the layers in soil?

Soil layers are even more complex, as you can see if you cut down through a section of soil. To do this geographers usually dig a 'soil pit'. This shows that soil is divided into layers or **horizons**. The cutting through the soil in photo **B** was done by natural erosion.

Vegetation

A horizon – mainly made from dead vegetation that is being broken down to form humus

Fantastic Facts

- Almost all the food we eat, the fibres for the clothes we wear, and timber for the houses we live in, are produced from soil.
- A single shovelful of soil can contain more species (kinds) of organisms (living things) than live above ground in the entire Amazon rainforest.
- One cup of soil may hold as many bacteria as there are people on Earth – that's over 6 billion!

OVER TO YOU

1 Look at diagram **C**, showing the links in an ecosystem. There are 11 links between the different parts of the system (numbered 1–11). These 11 links are listed below the diagram.

Match each link to one of the numbers. For example: 'Rain is needed for plants to grow' shows how climate influences vegetation – so it matches number 3 on the diagram, which is the arrow linking climate and vegetation.

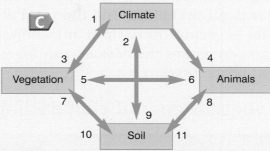

- Rain is needed for plants to grow
- Heavy rain can wash the soil away
- Transpiration from plant leaves makes the air more humid
- When it gets cold some animals hibernate
- Some plants grow best in acidic soils
- Soil provides a home, and a food supply, for burrowing animals
- Water is stored in the soil, which then evaporates and helps to form clouds and rain
- Plant roots bind the soil together and stop it being eroded
- When animals die they decay and add humus to the soil
- Animals help to spread seeds
- Bushes provide shelter for animals

2 Try to think of one more statement that could match each number.

Write these statements on a large copy of the diagram.

3 Diagram **D** shows a soil system.
  a On a copy of diagram **D**, label the A, B and C horizons. Write a sentence to describe each horizon.
  b The three main **inputs** into the soil system are weathered rock, dead organic matter and water. Mark each of these with an arrow: ➡ on your diagram. Label each arrow.
  c The following are movements in the soil. Mark each one with an arrow: ▬ ▬ ➡ on your diagram. Label each arrow.
  - Humus carried into the B horizon by organisms, like worms
  - Minerals carried down by water sinking through soil
  - Minerals carried up when evaporation draws water to surface
  - Soil washed away by erosion

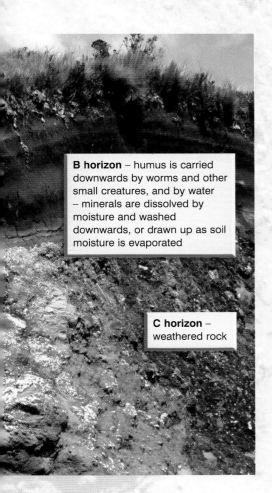

B horizon – humus is carried downwards by worms and other small creatures, and by water – minerals are dissolved by moisture and washed downwards, or drawn up as soil moisture is evaporated

C horizon – weathered rock

Why do rainforests grow so densely?

The rainforest can be described as 'the most productive ecosystem in the world'. This is because the heat, rainfall and sunlight give ideal conditions for plant growth. Trees and other plants grow rapidly, and the total amount of living material is greater here than anywhere else on Earth. You can see where the African rainforests grow by studying front cover resource *A*.

Total annual rainfall: 1354 mm

A

Climate graph for Kinshasa, Zaire 4°S

How are vegetation and climate linked?

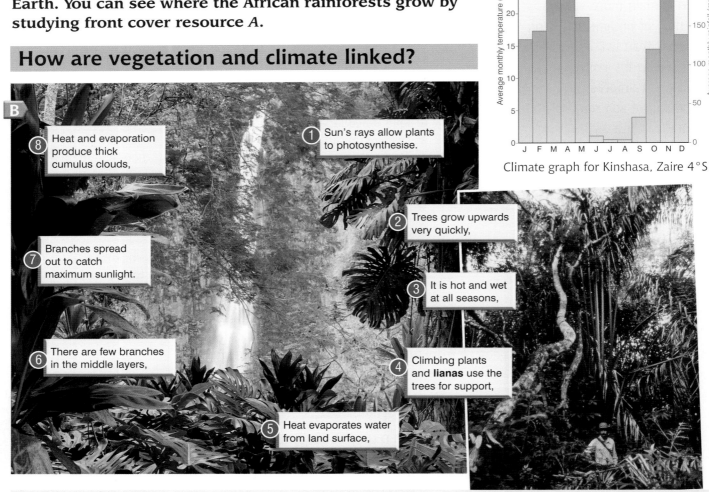

8 Heat and evaporation produce thick cumulus clouds,

1 Sun's rays allow plants to photosynthesise.

7 Branches spread out to catch maximum sunlight.

2 Trees grow upwards very quickly,

3 It is hot and wet at all seasons,

6 There are few branches in the middle layers,

4 Climbing plants and **lianas** use the trees for support,

5 Heat evaporates water from land surface,

1 Look at climate graph **A**.

Describe the main features of the climate. Refer to:
- high and low temperatures
- rainfall totals
- seasonal pattern
- length of growing season.

Hint: Most plants grow when the average temperature is higher than 7°C, and when there is moisture available in the soil.

2 Each of the 'tails' below can be added to one of the 'heads' on photo **B**. Match the heads and tails and then use the complete labels on your own copy of photo **B**.

a This produces new plant material.
b and transpires water from leaves.
c which bring rain storms.
d so plants grow all year round.
e so that they can compete for the light.
f to help them reach the light more quickly.
g They form a continuous **canopy**.
h because the canopy traps most of the sunlight.

70

How are vegetation and climate linked to the soil?

The rainforest vegetation is thick and luxuriant. It seems obvious, then, that the soil must be deep and fertile to support the forest.

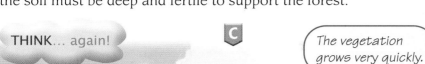

THINK... again!

C

The vegetation grows very quickly.

The climate is hot and damp.

What happens to all the dead plant and animal material as soon as it falls to the ground?

D

Rainfall is very heavy.

A lot of this rainwater sinks into the ground.

The water is warm.

When rain is so heavy that it cannot all sink into the soil, what will happen?

Will chemical weathering of the minerals in the soil be fast or slow?

Where will the water take the minerals that it weathers from the soil?

Key Words!

Lianas

Tall, thin plants that wind around the trees and use them as support to reach up to the canopy for sunlight.

Canopy

A tangle of branches and leaves from different trees, high above the forest floor, designed to catch the sunlight.

Fauna

The animals that live in an ecosystem.

OVER TO YOU

3 Think through the mind maps **C** and **D** above.

When you have come to some conclusions, label a copy of diagram **E** showing a rainforest soil.

4 So far you have studied rainforest climate, vegetation and soils, but there is also a rich animal and bird life ('**fauna**').

Work out, and explain why, the rainforest fauna is mainly in the canopy of the trees or in the rivers, and why so little lives on the forest floor. Use as many words and phrases from this word bank as you can.

- monkeys ● parrots ● snakes ● jaguars
- sloths ● fish ● crocodiles ● fruit ● nuts
- decay quickly ● light and heat ● safety
- fructivores (fruit eaters) ● carnivores (meat eaters)
- prey ● nutrients washed from soil into the rivers

E

What causes Africa's grasslands?

As you move away from the equator the climate changes, and so does the vegetation (see how it changes, on front cover resource A). Rainfall all year round gives way to seasonal rainfall; rainforest is replaced by savanna grassland. This leads to an environment that supports some of the most spectacular wildlife on the whole planet. If you are going to understand why the wildlife has developed you need to understand the climate, vegetation and soils in the ecosystem.

C

The vegetation shown in photos **A** and **B** has adapted to conditions of seasonal rainfall. The plants in this area have to survive a long period of hot, dry conditions (see graph **H**). They all have one or more ways of coping with the drought. They:

- seek water supplies, with long, deep roots
- cut down water loss by having small leaves, or waxy coatings on their leaves
- store water in thick trunks
- lie dormant during the dry season, and burst into life again as soon as the rainy season starts.

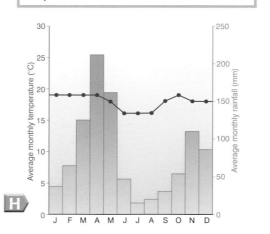

Climate graph for Nairobi, Kenya
(1820 m above sea level) **H**

D

E

Savanna grassland

1. Study graph **H**.
   a. Describe the climate. You should refer to:
      - highest temperature and lowest temperature
      - seasonal pattern of temperature
      - total rainfall
      - seasonal pattern of rainfall.
   b. Explain why the climate causes problems for plant growth.

2. Study photos **A** and **B** and diagrams **C–G** around it.
   a. In which season were the photos taken? (*Hint*: Was it the beginning of the wet season? The end of the dry season?) Explain your answer.
   b. Describe five ways in which plants in this scene are adapted to the climate.
   c. Explain how the features you described in **b** help the plants to deal with problems of the climate.

3. Why is this area so attractive to large herds of herbivorous (grass-eating) animals? Why is it so attractive to carnivores (flesh-eating animals) too?

4. a. How does the grass help to produce a humus-rich soil in this area?
   b. How do the animals help with this?

5. Suggest why these large herds have to migrate as the seasons change.

6. Why does this vegetation attract cattle herders to live in the area? But why does this cause problems for these herders?

OVER TO YOU

Why is tropical rainfall seasonal?

The equatorial rainforest region has rainfall at all seasons. As you move away from the equator the rainfall has a seasonal pattern, with a season of heavy rain and a season of drought. Why is this?

In the United Kingdom, the days get longer in summer and shorter in winter. This is because of the tilt of the Earth. In the northern summer, the Earth is tilted towards the sun, so the northern hemisphere receives more of the sun's rays, and days are longer than the nights. In December the northern hemisphere is tilted away from the sun, so the UK receives less of the sun's heat. It gets colder and our days are shorter.

The tilt of the Earth makes it seem as if the sun is moving to the north and south. The sun is not always overhead at the equator. So the area of heavy rainfall caused by the overhead sun moves north and south as the seasons change. It moves north of the equator in the northern summer. Then it moves south of the equator in the southern summer.

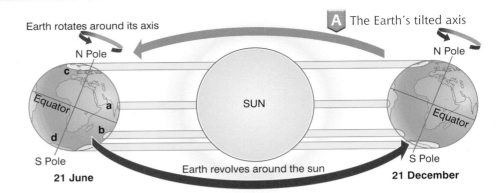

A The Earth's tilted axis

Earth rotates around its axis

N Pole

Equator

SUN

Earth revolves around the sun

21 June | 21 December

N Pole

Equator

S Pole | S Pole

a Sun shines directly down, so rays are concentrated. Land gets hot. Northern summer
b Rays strike at an angle, so heat is spread out. Southern winter
c Tilted towards sun: 24 hours of sunlight at midsummer
d Tilted away from sun: 24 hours of darkness at midwinter

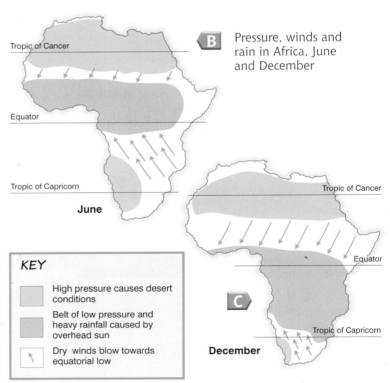

B Pressure, winds and rain in Africa, June and December

Tropic of Cancer

Equator

Tropic of Capricorn

June

KEY

High pressure causes desert conditions

Belt of low pressure and heavy rainfall caused by overhead sun

Dry winds blow towards equatorial low

C

Tropic of Cancer

Equator

Tropic of Capricorn

December

D Lusaka	Jan	Feb	Mar	Apr	May	Jun	Jul	Aug	Sep	Oct	Nov	Dec
Rainfall (mm)	231	191	142	18	3	2	1	0	2	10	91	150
Temperature (°C)	21	22	21	21	19	16	16	18	22	24	23	22

E Timbuktu	Jan	Feb	Mar	Apr	May	Jun	Jul	Aug	Sep	Oct	Nov	Dec
Rainfall (mm)	0	0	3	2	5	23	79	81	38	3	1	0
Temperature (°C)	22	24	28	32	34	35	32	30	32	31	28	23

OVER TO YOU

1 Using the figures in **D** and **E**, draw two graphs to show the climates of Timbuktu and Lusaka.

2 Cut out your graphs and stick them onto a map of Africa in the correct locations (you may need to draw an arrow to each place).

3 Describe the seasonal distribution of rainfall at Timbuktu, and at Lusaka.

4 Study maps **B** and **C**.
a When is the equatorial low pressure belt overhead at Timbuktu?
b When is it overhead at Lusaka?
c Why does it move like this?

5 Explain the link between the movement of the low pressure belt and the seasonal pattern of rainfall in Timbuktu and Lusaka.

6 What is the lowest temperature at Timbuktu, and at Lusaka?

7 Plant growth stops when the temperature of any month falls below 7°C.
a Does it ever become too cold for plant growth in tropical areas like Timbuktu and Lusaka?
b Why might plants in these areas have a season when they stop growing?
c For each place, when will that season be?

8 a Explain why soils on the savanna are often rich in humus.
b Why are savanna soils richer than rainforest soils?
c Where are all the nutrients:
● in the rainforest?
● in the savanna?

What are tropical grassland soils like?

Grasses are adapted to survive in a climate with two very different seasons.

Rainfall totals in Africa **F**

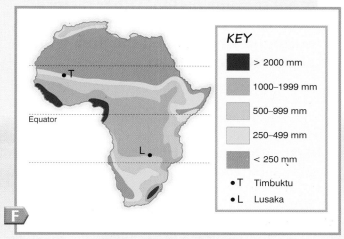

KEY
> 2000 mm
1000–1999 mm
500–999 mm
250–499 mm
< 250 mm
● T Timbuktu
● L Lusaka

Equator

G

Large herds of animals graze on the grasses. Their manure recycles nutrients into the soil.

In the wet season ...
● Grass grows quickly because temperatures are high. There is lots of moisture and sunlight for photosynthesis.
● Grass from the previous season decays slowly, and is carried into the soil by burrowing animals, worms, termites, etc. making the soil quite fertile.

In the dry season ...
● All plant growth stops because of a lack of moisture.
● The grass dies down and forms a thick mat which protects the roots from the heat of the sun.

Savanna grasslands – natural, or not?

Look back at diagram *A* on page 68. It shows that there are many interconnections between the different elements of ecosystems. Now look back to pages 72–73 to see how the savanna vegetation is adapted to the climate. The seasonal drought helps to explain why there are so few trees in this region, *but it is not the only reason!* Other factors need to be taken into account. One ecologist who studied the area wrote about this (extract *A*).

The Serengeti National Park [see map **D** on page 79] has areas of open plains, and areas of woodland. Scattered throughout the landscape are a few very large, old acacia trees that began life in a burst of growth in 1900. Spread throughout the park are areas of dense bush and trees that began life in a similar burst during the late 1970s. This is a story of disease and hunting, weather, and illegal poaching, and is one of the most dramatic stories of the ecology in Serengeti.

The life of the average tree is extremely difficult in the Serengeti, with all the animals it contains. This difficulty means that there are only rare times when trees can flourish and grow. While there are many factors which threaten the growth of trees, the two most important appear to be fires and grazing by animals.

Fire kills young trees. However, many of the tree species that grow on the savanna develop a thick bark as they grow older, and this bark can protect them from fire. So trees like the acacia need several years without fire to become established. Once they reach a certain age they are fine, and can survive most fires.

Fire is common on the savanna during the dry season. Some grass fires are natural, started by lightning. Others are started by herdsmen, who burn the dead grass at the end of the dry season. They do this so that their cattle can reach the new shoots more easily when they start to grow in the wet season. Grass shoots grow quickly, soon after a fire. Grass plants are not destroyed by fire as tree seedlings are.

Grazing also kills young trees. The main problem is not cattle, or small wild animals like zebra, wildebeest and deer. It is elephants. They can tear up trees that are up to about four years old. They find them more nutritious than grass. The young saplings are also easier for elephants to digest.

So what happened around 1900 and 1970 to allow trees to grow?

PASSPORT TO THE WORLD

Would you like to work in a National Park like Serengeti? It is obviously fair that local people have first choice of the jobs available, but you could gain experience of work like this by volunteering to work with an organisation like VSO or Farm Africa. They prefer volunteers who can offer some useful skills, so the best time to apply is when you have finished your higher education – but you could start thinking and planning now.

Fantastic Facts

Today, the Serengeti National Park, the Ngorongoro Conservation Area, and the Maasai Mara Game Reserve across the border in Kenya, protect the greatest and most varied collection of terrestrial wildlife on Earth. As a result, one of the last great migratory systems is still intact. Every October and November, over a million wildebeest and about 200 000 zebras flow south from the northern hills to the southern plains for the short rains. They then swirl west and north after the long rains in April, May and June. So strong is the ancient instinct to move that no drought, gorge or crocodile-infested river can hold them back.

1880	Big game hunting becomes popular in East Africa.
1890	Elephants are targeted by big game hunters, for their ivory.
1896	Rinderpest (a disease of cattle) first appears in East Africa.
1900	Rinderpest destroys native herds of cattle in Serengeti, then spreads to wild animals, especially wildebeest.
1900	Elephants are completely wiped out in Serengeti.
1902	Nomadic herders almost completely abandon Serengeti.
1910	Cattle numbers start to recover from rinderpest.
1930	The first elephants re-enter Serengeti from the south.
1940	Nomadic herders move back into Serengeti.
1951	Serengeti is declared a National Park.
1960	Elephants are now widespread in Serengeti.
1970	Wildebeest herds back to size they were before rinderpest outbreak. Poaching of elephants by local villagers becomes widespread.
1976	Start of series of years when rainy season becomes more spread out, making burning of grass more difficult. Park authorities enforce strict control on elephant poaching.
1989	Worldwide ban on trade in ivory.
1990	Park authorities control burning of grass – strip-burning stops fires spreading too far and too fast.
2000	Number of impala in park increases rapidly, mainly around new wooded areas.
1990–2005	Increasing pressure on Serengeti caused by population growth in areas around the park.

C

OVER TO YOU

1 Use the information in **C** to complete a living graph of the trees in Serengeti. Your teacher will provide you with a graph showing the ages of the trees.

2 Give two reasons why many trees in Serengeti date from about 1900.

3 Give two reasons why a lot more date from the late 1970s.

4 Give two reasons why few trees date from the period between 1910 and 1970.

5 Give one reason why new trees have grown in some areas since 1990.

6 Why might population growth in the areas around Serengeti stop the growth of new trees in future?

7 Suggest why the number of impala has increased recently.

8 Choose *one* of the changes you have described in your answers to questions 2–7. Draw a flow diagram to show how changing one aspect of the ecosystem has had knock-on effects on other aspects of the ecosystem.

9 Evaluate all the evidence you have seen about the causes of the savanna grasslands, and then decide – are the grasslands natural, or not?

 **WEBLINKS** **You will find a link to the Serengeti National Park at** www.nelsonthornes.com/horizons

Can the savanna ecosystem be conserved?

You have seen how people influence the ecosystem. They affect plants, animals and the soil in many different ways. However, people are also a part of the ecosystem. They *interact* with all the other elements.

On the last two pages you saw what happens to acacia trees when the number of elephants increases – they stop growing.

You also saw what happens to the impala when the number of acacia trees increases – they increase.

Conservationists in Serengeti National Park are trying to keep the different species of plants and animals in balance... but the whole ecosystem can be upset and changed if the number of people living in and around the park increases.

Serengeti is a National Park. The rules about this National Park are very different from those for a National Park in the UK. Most of the land is owned by the government, and there are very strict rules about who is allowed to live there and what they are allowed to do.

- Only Maasai people can live in Serengeti.
- They are only allowed there if they follow their traditional life as **nomads**.
- The numbers of people, and cattle, who can live there are strictly limited.

A Population statistics for Tanzania

	Total population	Birth rate/ thousand	Death rate/ thousand	Population growth %
1997	29 600 000	46	15	3.1
2004	36 600 000	39	17	2.2

B Total population of Serengeti, Loliondo district

1984	**1990**	**1996**	**2002**	**2005**
18 000	24 000	30 000	38 000	42 000

Key Words!

Nomads

People who move from place to place with no fixed home. They often live in areas with very different seasons, and move to find new pastures.

Pastoral farmers

– keep animals but do not grow crops.

Subsistence farmers

– mainly grow food for their own use.

Impala among acacia trees **C**

OVER TO YOU

1 a Draw a graph to show the rate of increase of Tanzania's population.

b Draw another graph to show the rate of increase in Serengeti-Loliondo.

c Describe the rates of increase shown on your two graphs.

d Compare the rates of increase on the two graphs.

e Look again at how Serengeti/Loliondo is changing. The increasing population has to live around the edges of the National Park. How will this be affecting the local ecosystems?

2 Study the three rules about people living in Serengeti National Park.

Evaluate these rules. Do you think they are **a** sensible and **b** fair?

The increased numbers of people who are living in Loliondo Wildlife Conservation Area (WCA) have several ways of making a living. These include:

- nomadic **pastoral farming**
- settled, **subsistence farming**, growing crops of maize or beans, and possibly keeping some cattle
- working in the tourist industry with either photo safari or hunting safari holidays
- hunting wild animals for food.

Using land for 'hunting tourism' can bring a total of $385/km² to the people living in the area (fees for overnight stays in villages, fees for guides, etc.) and bring profits to the tour companies. Numbers of hunters are limited – the government only issues a limited number of licences.

Using land for ecotourism 'camera safaris' can bring an income of between $500 and $835/km².

Poaching (illegal hunting of wildlife for meat) can bring in extra income. However, if they are caught, poachers can be fined or imprisoned, or even lose their rights to live in the Loliondo WCA.

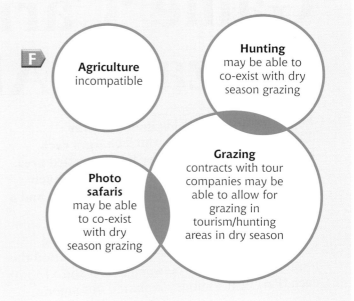
Serengeti National Park in Tanzania

E

Rainfall (approx.)	1000 mm	800 mm	600 mm	500 mm
Yield from maize ($/km²)	23 000	8000	400	0
Yield from cattle grazing ($/km²)	2100	1600	800	400

3 What would be the most economic way for Maasai people living in Loliondo to make a living if the rainfall was:
- about 1000 mm/year?
- about 500 mm/year?

4 What would the approximate rainfall be in a place where maize farming and cattle grazing yield about the same?

5 Study Venn diagram **F**.
- **a** Suggest why agriculture cannot exist on the same land as the other activities.
- **b** Suggest why grazing, hunting and photo safaris can all take place on at least some of the same land.

6 The Loliondo WCA authorities want to conserve as much wildlife as possible.

In areas where growing maize and grazing cattle bring in about the same amount of money (and support the same number of people), which should the WCA encourage?

Justify your answer.

7 Imagine that you are on a photo safari in the Loliondo-Serengeti area of Tanzania.

OVER TO YOU

Write an illustrated diary to describe your experiences.

You could find out more information by using the weblink below.

F

Agriculture incompatible

Hunting may be able to co-exist with dry season grazing

Grazing contracts with tour companies may be able to allow for grazing in tourism/hunting areas in dry season

Photo safaris may be able to co-exist with dry season grazing

Animals, people, or sustainable ecosystems?

Can the hunting and killing of wild animals ever be justified? In 1989 the world trade in ivory was banned. The main reason for this was to put a stop to the illegal poaching of elephants in Africa, including the Serengeti National Park. Yet still the killing of wildlife goes on.

A

You may feel that it was God, or nature, or evolution, that created the savanna ecosystem. However it was created, we have no right to kill any of the creatures in it.

B

the East African

4 February 2002

Game 'Carnage' in Tanzania Alarms Kenya

Safari hunting earns big money for the Tanzanian government, which charges each hunter $1600 a day to enter the controlled area. A hunter is also required to pay fees for each kill, with an elephant costing $4000, a lion and a leopard $2000 each, and a buffalo $600.

The sport is organised in expeditions lasting between one and three weeks. For the period the hunters stay they pay between $7270 and $13 170 each. Part of this money is shared out among the local villages, the local district councils and the central government.

Although the government restricts the number of animals to be shot, poor monitoring of the activities has meant indiscriminate killing of game, local community members told *The East African* during a recent trip to the area.

Kenyan wildlife conservation bodies are concerned that big game hunting in Tanzania is depleting the wildlife that crosses the border from Kenya.

C Most of the Maasai people who live in and on the edges of the Serengeti National Park and the Loloiondo Wildlife Conservation Area have a very low standard of living. We can only earn about $1/day. Hunting provides us with an additional source of food and income.

In a natural ecosystem there is a balance between predators and their prey (see graph **D**).

Tanzania is one of the poorest countries in the world. Any source of income should be valued.

In an average year, local people illegally kill about 40 000 animals, mainly wildebeest and zebra, but also giraffe, buffalo and impala. Many other animals are caught in poachers' snares or pit fall traps.

Only kill for food; never for sport.

Migration is an essential part of the life cycle of the animals of the savanna. If hunters are allowed to disrupt that cycle by killing animals in one area, they will affect the whole ecosystem of a much larger area.

If you don't support hunting as a way of providing food you are a hypocrite … unless you are also a vegetarian.

A simple ecosystem with two species: one predator and one prey

D

KEY
— No. of prey species
— No. of predator species

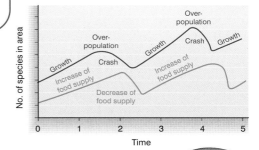

Sensible management of the animal reserves must involve some culling of species to keep the system in balance. If people are willing to pay to help the culling we should take advantage of their money.

OVER TO YOU

1 In a natural savanna ecosystem there is a balance between grass, wildebeest and lions.
a Explain what would happen to wildebeest and lions if:
- a drought reduced the amount of grass one year
- more rainfall increased the amount of grass one year.

b Explain what would happen to grass and lions if:
- a disease reduced the number of wildebeest by 50 per cent
- game wardens protected the wildebeest from human hunters, so their numbers rose by 20 per cent.

2 Choose one of the following roles.
- Maasai cattle herder who lives in Serengeti
- Tanzanian government official who issues licences for hunting game in Loliondo Wildlife Conservation Area
- camera safari tourist
- Serengeti game warden who has the job of conserving the savanna ecosystem
- local politician who wants to encourage tourism in Tanzania

Explain your attitude to hunting wild animals for sport and/or for food.

In your answer you *must* refer to the whole ecology of the savanna grasslands.

3 Organise a debate in your class between people with different views on hunting wild animals.

'Should hunting of wild animals ever be allowed in the Serengeti or Loliondo areas of Tanzania?'

Some of you might be given particular roles by your teacher and asked to start off the debate. The other people in the class should offer their views later.

Try to reach a conclusion that all the class can agree with.

If you cannot all agree, try to find a solution that a large majority agrees with.

Where are we now?

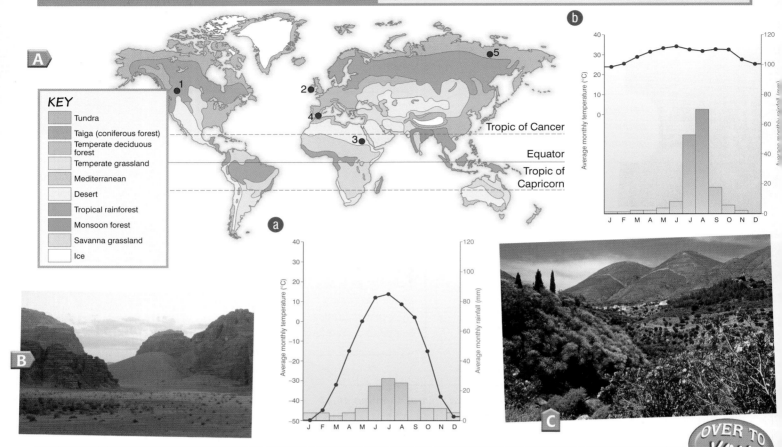

KEY

- Tundra
- Taiga (coniferous forest)
- Temperate deciduous forest
- Temperate grassland
- Mediterranean
- Desert
- Tropical rainforest
- Monsoon forest
- Savanna grassland
- Ice

G

- Plants with seeds that can lie dormant for several years, waiting for rainfall to allow them to germinate
- Rich brown soil, caused by the annual fall of leaves in autumn
- Poor soils, with little humus, because of the sparse vegetation cover
- Hot, dry summers and warm, wet winters, so the vegetation lies dormant in summer
- Has a short growing season, which means the trees keep their leaves through the winter, to save energy
- Deep, rich black soils, caused by the build-up of humus from the decay of grass
- Has a poor soil, because the leaves are tough and needle-like to protect them from the cold, so they only decay slowly
- Bulbs that flower in spring, because that is the only season when sunlight can penetrate through the branches of the trees
- Areas around the Mediterranean have been farmed for thousands of years, so the soils are often eroded and worn out
- A season of rainfall and a season of drought that makes tree growth difficult, but allows rich grassland to develop

---

OVER TO YOU

1. Study the five climate graphs, **a–e**.
   a. Write a brief description of the climate at each place.
   b. Link the five climates to the locations on the map, marked 1 to 5.

2. Study the five photos **B–F**.
   a. Write a description of the aspects of the ecosystem (vegetation, soils, animals, etc.) that you can see in the photos.
   b. Match the photos to the places and the climates that you linked in question 1.

3. Read the ten statements in panel **G** about the five ecosystems.

   Divide them into two groups:
   a. five that describe and explain the vegetation and
   b. five that describe and explain the soil.

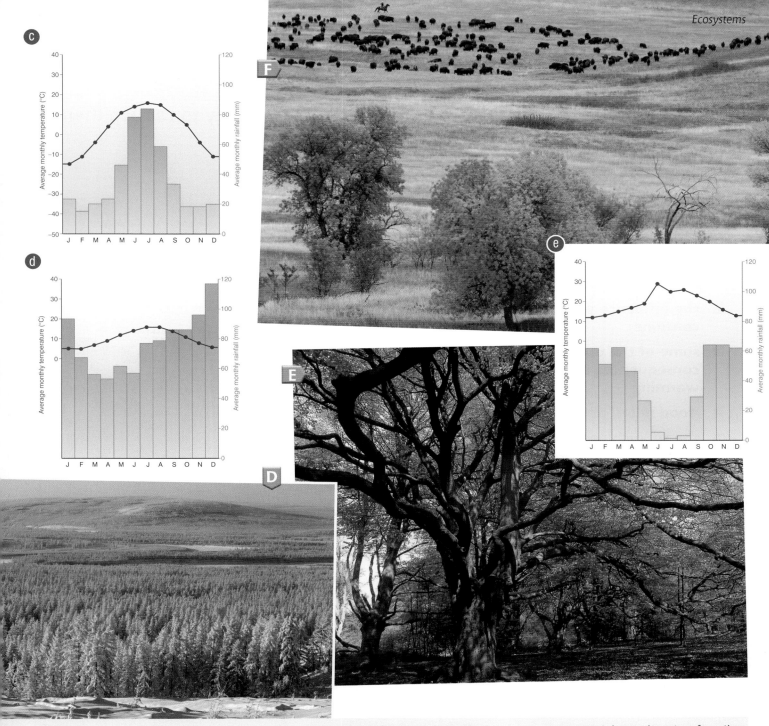

4 Choose two statements, one from group **a** and one from group **b** in question 3, to describe each of the new ecosystems shown on the map (that is, not including tropical rainforest and savanna grassland).

5 Work in groups. Make a display on a large world map outline. Illustrate the seven ecosystems that you have studied in this unit

(tropical rainforest and savanna grassland, as well as the five that you have looked at on these two pages).

Some of you may decide to describe the ecosystems, using the photos and the statistics. Some of you may take your studies of these ecosystems further. You may carry out an enquiry into issues linked to the ecosystems. For instance:

● How might exploration for oil in Alaska affect the tundra ecosystem?
● Coniferous forests are an important source of wood for building and for industry, but can these forests be managed in a sustainable way?
● Why have the prairie grasslands become the world's major wheat-growing areas?

And so on.

5 Think – Act

Think about your global footprints ... Act locally to reduce them

Where are we going?

In this unit you will learn about the way that we all leave our 'footprints' on the global environment. You will see that, as individuals, we cannot stop all the damage to the global environment – but we can take local actions that will help. You will learn about:

- the influence you have on the environment when you *consume*

- some of the causes and consequences of global warming

- 'food miles' and 'ghost acres'

- the rubbish problem

- what we can all do to reduce the size of our footprints on the global environment.

C

Last summer Francesca had thought about her global connections after she had studied *Horizons 2* Passport to the World pages 124–125. Here she is, getting breakfast. Follow her connections on these pages and through the rest of Unit 5. She thinks about her global connections and then tries to reduce the damage that she is doing to the environment of the planet.

B

H

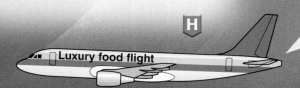

Luxury food flight

Links to... Look back to *Horizons 1*, page 15. There you learned about Jacob and his global connections. Now you need to think about how our global connections affect the world.

D

F

G

A

E

1 Describe Francesca's global connections.

2 Explain how Francesca is affecting the world when she consumes her breakfast.

3 Draw mind maps to show and explain her connections.

4 Think of yourself and your connections and the way you affect the global ecosystem. You could draw mind maps to show the effects of:
- your journey to school
- the clothes and shoes that you buy and wear
- the water you drink, and the waste water that flows out of your house

and so on.

5 a With a partner, look at your results for activity 4. Try to suggest ways of reducing your impact on the environment.

b Compare your ideas with the ideas of another pair of pupils. Evaluate each suggestion, thinking about how it would reduce your impact on the environment and whether it would cause costs or inconvenience to you.

OVER TO YOU

What is global warming?

One of the connections from Francesca's breakfast showed an iceberg forming in the Antarctic, thousands of miles away from her home. How and why is Francesca's breakfast connected to this iceberg? And how are they connected to flooding in Bangladesh, and to erosion of the coast in eastern England?

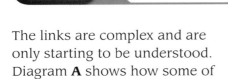 **Links to...** To remind you of these two topics, go to *Horizons 1* Unit 4 and *Horizons 2* Unit 1.

The links are complex and are only starting to be understood. Diagram **A** shows how some of those links work.

Most scientists and geographers agree that global warming is taking place, and most of them agree about some of the causes. Even so, a lot of research is still needed to find out:

- Just what is global warming?
- How will it affect us?
- Can it be slowed down or even stopped?

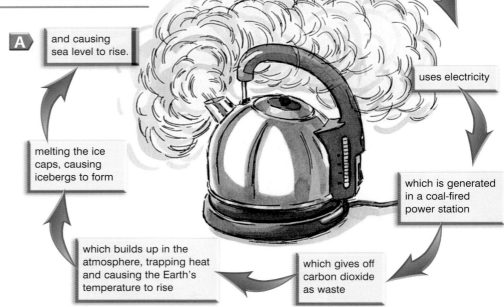

A and causing sea level to rise.

Boiling the kettle

uses electricity

which is generated in a coal-fired power station

which gives off carbon dioxide as waste

melting the ice caps, causing icebergs to form

which builds up in the atmosphere, trapping heat and causing the Earth's temperature to rise

Here are some of the changes that have been linked to global warming.

- The Earth is getting hotter.
- The 10 hottest years ever recorded have been in the period since 1990.
- The world's climate seems to be more unstable.
- Areas like the Caribbean and the southern states of the USA are having more, and worse, hurricanes than ever before.
- The UK seems to be having more periods of very dry weather – and more periods of wet weather and flooding.
- Sea level is rising all over the world.
- Glaciers are retreating and the polar ice sheets are shrinking.

Fantastic Facts

- Between 1900 and 2000 the Earth's average temperature increased by 0.5°C.
- Between 1980 and 2000 the Earth's average temperature increased by 0.3°C.
- Since 1900, average sea level has risen by about 10 cm.

If you project these figures forward for the rest of your lifetime, they look serious.

In the past few years it has become obvious that global warming is causing the great Antarctic ice sheet to melt more quickly. This can be seen in photos **B** of the Larsen B ice sheet, which collapsed in 2002.

This shows the Larsen B ice shelf floating on the sea, with part of the solid land of the Antarctic Peninsula on the left. In January (late summer) the ice shelf is dotted with meltwater pools. By mid-February, about 800 km² has broken off the ice sheet and floated out to sea as icebergs. Then, in early March, another 1800 km² collapses to form 'sliver icebergs' and 'bergy bits'. This was one of the biggest, fastest break-ups of ice sheets that had ever been witnessed.

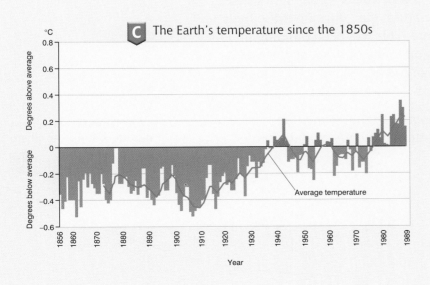

Scale: 1 mm = 1 km (approx)

B

| 31 January 2002 | Mid-February 2002 | 5 March 2002 | 7 March 2002 |

1 Study graph **C**.
a Write a brief comment to describe the Earth's average temperature in these decades:
- 1910s ● 1930s ● 1950s ● 1970s ● 1990s.
b What is the trend shown by these figures?
c If this trend continues, what is likely to happen to the Earth's temperature by:
- 2020? ● 2050? ● 2100?

2 How are these changes affecting the polar ice sheets?

Study photos **B**.
a Describe the changes in the ice shelf over this three-month period.
b Use the scale with the photos to work out roughly what area of ice broke away from the ice sheet.
c How will this affect sea level?

3 Use the weblink suggested below.

Work in groups of four, with each person choosing one of:
- UK
- Spain
- Switzerland
- Finland.
a Collect data and information to show how the climate of your chosen country might change during the next century.
b Explain how these changes might affect life in those countries.

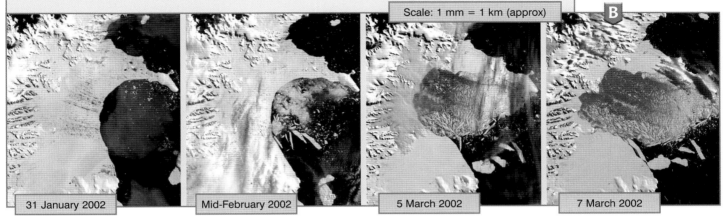

C The Earth's temperature since the 1850s

Year

WEBLINKS **You will find a link giving information on how the world climates may change, at** www.nelsonthornes.com/horizons

What is causing global warming?

Global warming is caused by an increase in carbon dioxide and other gases in the Earth's atmosphere. These gases make the atmosphere behave like a greenhouse. They let the sun's rays pass through, but then they trap a lot of the heat. This is making the Earth heat up.

Diagram **A** shows the natural process that has always operated. Diagram **B** shows changes to this process caused by the burning of fossil fuels in the last two centuries. You will notice that diagram **B** does not have many labels!

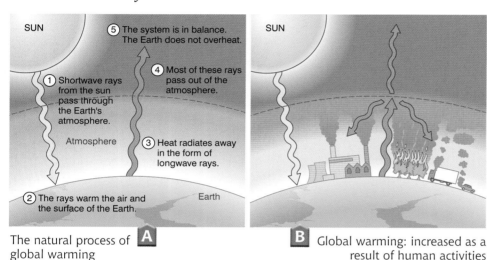

The natural process of global warming **A**

B Global warming: increased as a result of human activities

Since the Industrial Revolution, which began in the UK in about 1750, people have been burning more and more **fossil fuels** – coal at first, then growing amounts of petroleum, and then natural gas. Burning these fuels releases carbon dioxide into the atmosphere. This has been building up in the atmosphere. The 'greenhouse gases' stop many of the longwave rays from the Earth's surface passing back out of the atmosphere. This means that heat is trapped in the Earth system.

This has led to the rise in the average temperature that is melting the ice at the poles. It has also affected the world pattern of winds, making the weather less stable and less predictable.

Concentration of carbon dioxide in the atmosphere

C

1. Why do you think the process that leads to global warming is known as 'the greenhouse effect'?

2. Complete a copy of diagram **B**, to show how the burning of fossil fuels has led to the greenhouse effect.

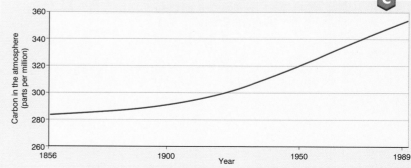

The carbon cycle

Coal was formed from the remains of forests that grew in swamps during the Carboniferous period.

The trees that grew in these forests had taken carbon from the atmosphere to help their growth. This carbon was stored in the structure of the tree. Then, when the tree died, the carbon was stored in the ground, and formed coal. Millions of years later the coal was mined and burnt to produce heat and power. The carbon from the coal was released. It combined with oxygen from the air to form carbon dioxide.

Carbon dioxide is not the only greenhouse gas. Table **D** shows how other processes produce, and use up, greenhouse gases.

D

These processes *increase* greenhouse gases		These processes *reduce* greenhouse gases
Burning fossil fuels	CO_2	• Soil formation, where plant remains become part of soil
Manufacture of cement	CO_2	
Deforestation	CO_2	• Growth of biomass – including trees – with carbon in their structure
Increased rice production in padi fields	methane	
Digestion of grass by cattle	methane	• Formation of bone and shell ($CaCO_3$)
Domestic sewage + landfill	methane	
Industrial production	CFCs etc.	

OVER TO YOU

3 Compare graph **C** with graph **C** on page 87. Do they seem to be linked? Explain your answer.

4 Draw a diagram to show the 'carbon cycle'. Your diagram should show how carbon can go:
- from atmosphere to vegetation
- from vegetation to rock
- from rock to power station
- from power station to atmosphere

and so on.

5 Explain why cement manufacture can add carbon dioxide to the atmosphere.

Hint: Limestone is one of the main raw materials for cement. It has to be heated during manufacture.

6 When you have answered questions 4 and 5, use your answer to draw a 'carbon cycle' diagram for cement manufacture.

7 Processes that 'soak up' carbon dioxide and reduce the greenhouse effect are sometimes called 'carbon sinks'. Explain how they work.

8 Work with a partner or in a small group.
- **a** Make up a list of ways that you contribute to global warming.
- **b** Sort your global warming activities into groups that probably contribute to the problem:
  - a lot
  - a little.
- **c** Consider each activity and evaluate how hard it would be to either give up or cut down on this activity.

How can we cut carbon emissions?

In 1997, at a conference in Kyoto, Japan, world leaders agreed that their countries would cut emissions of greenhouse gases. They said that, by 2012, they would reduce their emissions so that they were 5% below the 1990 figure.

Unfortunately, the Kyoto Agreement has been through many difficulties since then. The main problem is that the USA has refused to ratify the agreement. Other countries thought that this was unfair and would give the USA an unfair advantage. Non-polluting, 'green' energy is more expensive.

However, after a lot of negotiating, about 100 countries have signed up to the Kyoto Agreement, so the world has made a start on reducing its emissions of greenhouse gases.

The UK had actually been making quite good progress on reducing emissions, as graph **A** shows.

Then, in March 2005, the UK government announced the country's emission figures for 2003.

Emissions of carbon dioxide – the main greenhouse gas – jumped by 2.2% or 3.4 million tonnes of carbon. The big increases are largely a result of power companies switching back to coal following rises in gas prices.

A Friends of the Earth climate campaigner said:

Unless we take control of UK emissions and start delivering substantial year-on-year reductions, this target will be impossible to reach. It's time to get a grip on climate change before it is too late.

B

Francesca can play her part in controlling emissions. So can you!

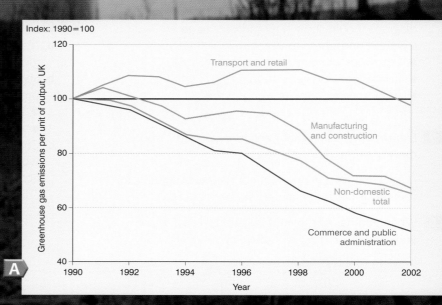

Index: 1990=100

Greenhouse gas emissions per unit of output, UK

Transport and retail

Manufacturing and construction

Non-domestic total

Commerce and public administration

Year

A Greenhouse gases – falls in most sectors

Here are some ways to save energy **in your house**:	Here are some ways to save energy **in transport**:
● double glaze or even triple glaze	● don't ask for a lift, but walk or cycle
● use low-energy light bulbs	● use public transport
● turn off the TV rather than leaving it on standby	● make sure that the car is serviced regularly
● use the energy-saving facility on the computer	● share your car with others – offer lifts to friends and colleagues
● insulate cavity walls and lofts	and you can probably think of more.
● stop draughts	
● lag the hot-water tank	
● turn down the thermostat	
and you can probably think of more.	

C

Can you think of ways that you could save energy **in school**?

OVER TO YOU

1 The caption for graph **A** states that there have been 'falls in most sectors'.

a Which sector increased its greenhouse gas emissions at first, and then started to reduce them?

b Which sector has shown the most rapid fall in the emissions of greenhouse gases?

c Suggest how emissions might have been reduced in this and other sectors.
In your answer you could use some or all of these words:

- ● insulation
- ● thermostats
- ● improved technology
- ● reduced travelling
- ● changing sources of power

d Name one major user of energy where emissions have *not* fallen.

Hint: It is not named on the graph, but there is a good clue if you study the graph carefully.

2 Use the weblink below to visit the Best Foot Forward site. It has a simple calculator, which you can use to work out approximately how much carbon *you* add to the atmosphere each year.

3 a What have you, and the other people in your household, done to reduce the energy use in your house, and to cut greenhouse gas emissions?

b What *more* could you do?

Suggest sensible changes. Don't suggest making your house so cold that your granny suffers from hypothermia!

c Compare your suggestions with those of the rest of the class.

Try to agree a list of principles for all the members of the class to follow at home, so that you can all cut your greenhouse emissions together.

d Explain why 'cutting your greenhouse emissions together' could be seen as being a bit like the Kyoto Agreement.

4 Work through the same three stages that you did in activity 3 – but this time think about your use of energy in transport.

a What have you done already?

b What more could you do?

c Make a list of class principles.

You could visit the Sustrans website to help with this (see the weblink below).

5 a Working as a class, draw up some energy-saving rules (or advice) for your school.
Include suggestions for travel to school as well as your time in school.

b Design a series of posters for school, to show your energy-saving rules, or advice.

Hint: Someone could design a basic outline of a poster on the computer. Then the rest of the class can develop that design to give a series of messages – just like a real publicity campaign.

When you have designed a set of posters, plan an energy-saving campaign. You should consider:

- ● where to put the posters for maximum effect
- ● whether to back up the posters with a newsletter
- ● whether to introduce the campaign with a presentation in assembly
- ● whether you need to discuss energy saving with the school caretaker, or with the member of staff who has responsibility for paying the bills
- ● whether it might be worth contacting the local press about your campaign
- ● how your campaign might link to work in Citizenship, Science, etc.

and so on.

c Display the posters around the class. Evaluate each other's posters. You need to assess them against the following criteria:

- ● the layout should be clear and striking
- ● the content of the message should be clear, relevant to the audience and accurate
- ● the overall impression should make the audience want to take action.

WEBLINKS | **You will find a link to the Best Foot Forward and Sustrans sites at** www.nelsonthornes.com/horizons

How does our food affect the environment?

On page 84 Francesca was having orange juice for breakfast. The juice came from Brazil. So how is that orange juice affecting the size of her environmental footprint?

Let's start by thinking about school dinners! To some of you that might bring pleasant images to mind. Other people may have less attractive images.

Many people have been concerned about the nutritional standards of some school meals. They say that there should be more fresh fruit and vegetables, and less fat and sugar in the meals. More food should be bought in fresh and less processed food should be served.

Some schools are taking action to improve their school meals by buying as much food as possible from the local area.

Orton Primary School in Cumbria has a 'Local Food Procurement Officer'. She talked to parents about the diet they preferred for their children. As a result, processed foods are now *out* and local, seasonal food is *in*, with an emphasis on traditional baking. Locally produced bacon and sausages, local lamb and bean casserole and traditionally baked ginger sponge have been huge successes.

This post has been funded by the Cumbria Fells and Dales Leader+ programme. Leader+ groups were set up as an experiment by the EU to look at new ways of developing rural areas. They provide funds for local people and companies to 'add value to local produce and to link livelihoods and landscapes'.

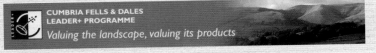

CUMBRIA FELLS & DALES LEADER+ PROGRAMME
Valuing the landscape, valuing its products

Other organisations supported by Leader+ include farmers' markets, food processing facilities and food trails.

WEBLINKS For details of the trails Ale Trail, Apple Appeal, Damson Valleys, Organic Origins, Sausage Secrets and Stone Settings, follow the links from www.nelsonthornes.com/horizons

1 How does the Orton Local School Food Procurement Officer help:
- children in the school
- local farmers
- local tradesmen?

2 Look back to *Horizons 1* pages 88–93. Suggest why the Aireys of Black Moss Farm might support a Local Food Procurement Officer in their local school.

3 Look back at *Horizons 2* pages 74–77.
  a Why might Luis Garcia be worried about Local Food Procurement Officers in British schools?
  b Why will locally produced food never be able to replace all the goods that Luis carries from Andalucia?

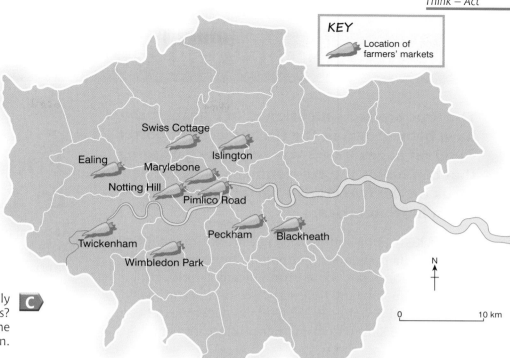

Swiss Cottage
Ealing
Islington
Marylebone
Notting Hill
Pimlico Road
Twickenham
Peckham
Blackheath
Wimbledon Park

N

0   10 km

Key Words!

Farmers' market

Here farmers, growers or producers from a defined local area are present in person to sell their own produce, direct to the public. All products sold should have been grown, reared, caught, brewed, pickled, baked, smoked or processed by the stallholder.

Are **farmers' markets** only found in small market towns? *No* – the map shows the farmers' markets in London.

WEBLINKS

For more details on farmers' markets in London and elsewhere, follow the links from www.nelsonthornes.com/horizons

One idea behind the growth of farmers' markets is to reduce the number of miles travelled by the food that reaches the consumer's plate. Cutting 'food miles' has many benefits for the environment.

4 Describe the distribution of farmers' markets in London.

5 Visit the farmers' market websites (see the weblink above).
  a Find the location of your nearest farmers' market.
  b Collect information from the website to show the main attractions of the markets for consumers and for farmers.

6 You have been asked by your local farmers' market to design either a poster or a PowerPoint presentation to show why the market is good for the environment. Your presentation should refer to some, or all, of:
- food miles
- reduced use of fuel
- reduced air pollution (including reduced carbon dioxide output)
- fresher food for fitter consumers
- supporting local farmers helps to maintain the traditional rural environment
- other ideas of your own.

OVER TO YOU

7 Evaluate the posters or the presentations from the members of the class. You need to set clear standards by which you will judge the work. Look back to activity 5 on page 91 to see how that was evaluated.

8 What about Francesca's orange juice? Could she reduce her footprint by buying juice from a farmers' market? Could you reduce your footprints by buying more local produce?

Are food miles only about energy?

The four products mentioned in extract *A could* have been grown in the UK but were imported – and on pages 92–93 you saw how damaging that can be for the environment. Now we will focus on the two crops – carrots and beans – flown in from Africa.

Neither Kenya nor South Africa produces enough food to feed all of its population. Yet both of these countries grow food for richer, more economically developed countries – using land that was once used for growing food for local people. Meanwhile, many people in those countries are suffering from malnutrition, or even starvation.

The land that no longer produces essential food for the local population is sometimes called the 'ghost acres'. So it is interesting to discover who is making the decisions when land becomes part of these ghost acres. In Kenya:

- 18% of the land growing vegetables for export is owned by small farmers
- 42% forms large commercial farms owned by rich individuals and families or by large Kenyan companies
- 40% is land owned by the transnational corporations, which are foreign-owned.

The export of fresh vegetables from sub-Saharan Africa to industrialised countries rose by 150% between 1989 and 1997. Since then the rate of increase has continued or even speeded up.

A

Food miles are big in the food aisles

It is early September. Home-grown seasonal fruit and vegetables like apples, onions, carrots and green beans are available throughout the country. But I visited three central London supermarkets and found they were selling:

- apples carried 7564 km from the USA
- onions carried 19 000 km from Australia and New Zealand
- carrots brought 8200 km from South Africa and
- beans flown 5793 km from Kenya.

B

Vegetables exported include:

Asparagus	Mangetout peas	Green beans
Runner beans	Baby carrots	Baby sweet corn
Brussels sprouts	Broccoli	Garden peas
Chillies	Artichokes	

Fruits exported include:

Avocados	Mangoes	Passion fruit
Pineapples	Melons	

More recently, cut **flowers**, especially roses, are also being grown and exported.

C Modern commercial farming in Kenya

D The facts: Kenya and the UK

		Kenya	UK
Calories/day (average per person)		2090	3412
% of children under 5 who are moderately or severely underweight		20.2	< 2
Undernourished people as a % of total population		33	< 2
Vegetables*:	Production	1206	2747
	Import	6	3386
	Export	53	275
Fruit*:	Production	1933	295
	Import	8	6095
	Export	122	276
Cereals*:	Production	2773	
	Import	725	
	Export	47	
Starchy roots (mainly cassava, potatoes and sweet potatoes*)			
	Production	2030	
	Import	3	
	Export	0	

* All figures in thousands of metric tonnes

Traditional subsistence farming in Kenya **E**

1
a What are 'ghost acres' in countries like Kenya and South Africa?
b Name two crops that are grown on the ghost acres.
c Are these **staple foods** or luxury foods?

F

N

AFRICA

Kenya

0   1000 km

Key Words!

Staple foods

Staple foods provide people with their main energy supply. They include cereals and starchy roots.

2
a Give three pieces of evidence which show that Kenya is not producing enough staple food for its population.
b Compare nutrition levels in Kenya with those in the UK.

3
a Give two pieces of evidence which show that Kenya is producing luxury foods to export to more economically developed countries – like the UK.
b Give two pieces of evidence which show that the UK does not rely heavily on Kenya for its imports of 'luxury' foods like fruit and vegetables.

4 Illustrate your answers to question 2 *or* 3 with a graph or diagram.

OVER TO YOU

5 Choose one person from list A below, and one from list B. For each of your choices write a statement to explain what you feel about the ghost acres in Kenya, where land that was once used for growing food for local people is now used for growing export crops.

List A
- Aid worker, working with malnourished children in a Kenyan village
- Farm labourer, who lost his land when he fell into debt to the bank
- Kenyan Minister for Health

List B
- Rich landowner who grows vegetables for export
- Chief buyer for fresh produce for a UK supermarket chain
- Kenyan Minister for Finance

Compare your answers with those written by other people in the class. Discuss how you could improve your answers.

Rubbish – what's the problem?

So far in this unit we have looked at the big issues of global warming and food miles. We have seen how people in this country can leave 'footprints' in other parts of the world because of what they consume. We have also tried to look at some of the ways we can reduce our footprints on the environment, by taking care with the way we consume.

First of all we should look at the scale of the problem in the UK ...

Unfortunately it is very difficult for us to see how our actions on these big issues are making a difference.

- It is all very well agreeing to walk to school – and not asking your parent for a lift – but then you see three lanes of traffic roaring up the motorway and you wonder why you bothered.

- It may make you feel good when you buy Brussels sprouts from a British farm rather than baby corn and mangetout peas from Kenya – but does the supermarket boss notice?

You can make a very obvious difference, though, by shopping carefully and taking care with what you throw away – and where you throw it! The waste packaging that Francesca is throwing away in photo **A** had connections to the rest of the world. So does *your* rubbish.

Now let's focus on one part of the country – West London. Dealing with rubbish from this area is the job of the West London Waste Authority (WLWA).

Fantastic Facts

General garbage
- The UK produces more than 434 million tonnes of waste every year. This rate of rubbish generation would fill the Albert Hall in London in less than 2 hours.
- Every year UK households throw away the equivalent of 3½ million double-decker buses (almost 30 million tonnes) – a queue of which would stretch from London to Sydney (Australia) and back.
- On average, each person in the UK throws away seven times their body weight (about 500 kg) in rubbish every year.

Statistics
The total authority area is 380 km² and the total population is 1 409 265. In 2002/03, the WLWA's area produced a total of 837 289 tonnes of municipal waste. Of this, 763 449 tonnes was household waste.

In 2001/02 over 768 000 tonnes of waste was transported from 17 transfer stations or Civic Amenity sites for disposal by landfill. 67% of this waste was transported to landfill by railway – mostly from the WLWA's two major transfer stations at Brentford and at South Ruislip – with the remainder going by road (except for about 1000 tonnes by river barge).

B West London Waste Authority

Harrow
Brent
Hillingdon
Ealing
Hounslow
Richmond upon Thames

N

0   10 km

KEY
○ Civic Amenity sites for public to bring waste

Location of landfill
31% of the waste went to landfill in Buckinghamshire, 35% to landfill in Bedfordshire, 32% to landfill in Oxfordshire and the remaining 2% to landfill in Surrey and Essex.

The WLWA has **statutory government targets**:
- to recycle/compost 18% of all household waste by 2003/04
- to recycle/compost 27% of all household waste by 2005/06.

1 The waste that is produced in an area like West London has costs. As a class, brainstorm all the ways that this waste causes:
- damage to the environment
- financial costs to the population.

2 Draw a map to show where the waste from West London is taken for disposal.

3 Use the figures for total waste production and for the amount that was sent to landfill sites, to work out what percentage of the area's waste is recycled.

4 What are the government's recycling targets for local authorities? Was West London close to those targets in 2002?

So how can I reduce my rubbish footprints?

There are three ways to start to reduce the damage that you do to the environment, and the cost of dealing with this damage. You can:

- reduce
- reuse
- recycle.

Reduce the amount of goods that you buy and then, if possible, **reuse** goods rather than throwing them away – but when you do throw them away try to make sure that they are sent for **recycling**.

For example, a huge amount of the waste from most households in the UK comes in the form of packaging and bags from our shopping, so …

- **Reduce** the amount of packaging that you use by:
  - ☺ taking a shopping bag with you so that you do not need to get a carrier bag from every shop
  - ☺ buying loose apples in a simple plastic bag, rather than packed by the supermarket in an elaborate plastic tray.
- **Reuse** your packaging by:
  - ☺ saving your supermarket carrier bags and taking them back next time you go shopping
  - ☺ saving bottles and jars and using them to store things around the house.
- **Recycle** by:
  - ☺ putting as much stuff out for separate collection by the bin men
  - ☺ learning where those things that the bin men do not collect for recycling, can be taken.

Fantastic Facts

Every year, an estimated 17.5 billion plastic bags are given away by British supermarkets. This is equivalent to over 290 bags for every person in the UK. A tax on plastic shopping bags in the Republic of Ireland has cut their use by more than 90% and raised millions of euros in revenue. The tax of 15 cents per bag was introduced in an attempt to curb litter, and the improvement was immediate. The 3.5 million euros in extra revenue raised so far will be spent on environmental projects.

5 Carry out a survey to find exactly how much packaging you throw away in your own households.

- **a** Classify your waste packaging into groups, such as paper, cardboard, glass, metal, plastic, etc.
- **b** Work out how much of this waste packaging you reuse and how much you recycle.
- **c** Complete a class survey to find out how much packaging you all use, reuse and recycle.
- **d** Work out how each person in the class can start to reduce his or her footprint, by suggesting one simple way of reducing that person's waste.

Evaluate the success of this enquiry.
- Were the results what you expected?
- How well did class members collect, present and analyse the information?
- Will the enquiry lead to action?

OVER TO YOU

C

Banish your bovver. boot footprint because …..

Cut your kitten heel footprint because …..

Reduce your Reebok footprint because …..

Rubbish – what's the solution?

Diagram *A* shows the theory of one type of recycling. The Closed Loop system operates in London. It involves very careful planning so that London councils know what types of waste to collect and where they will send them to be recycled. They also need to know exactly how the recycled materials can be used in the manufacturing industry.

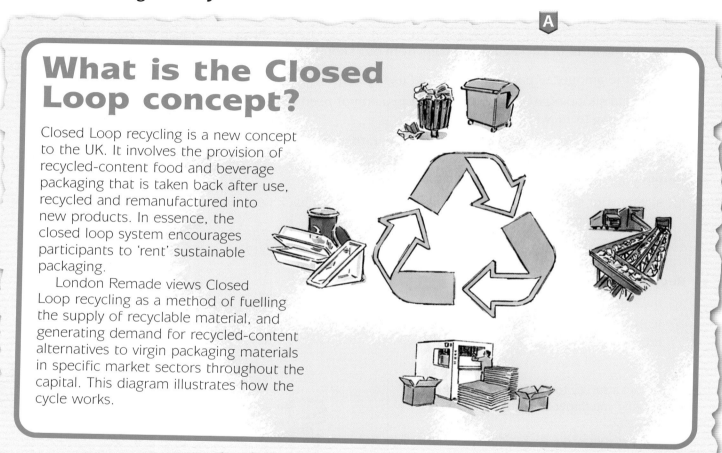

A

What is the Closed Loop concept?

Closed Loop recycling is a new concept to the UK. It involves the provision of recycled-content food and beverage packaging that is taken back after use, recycled and remanufactured into new products. In essence, the closed loop system encourages participants to 'rent' sustainable packaging.

London Remade views Closed Loop recycling as a method of fuelling the supply of recyclable material, and generating demand for recycled-content alternatives to virgin packaging materials in specific market sectors throughout the capital. This diagram illustrates how the cycle works.

A lot of effort has obviously been put into researching and planning this Closed Loop system in London. If you are going to reduce your own footprints, and the footprints of your community, you need to do a similar research and planning exercise.

1 List **B** names several types of waste that are collected for recycling in many parts of the UK.
  a As a class, draw up a directory to show where each of these products can be taken, or how they can be collected for recycling.

  b Draw a map of your area to show where the recycling collection points are for each of the products.
  c Discuss what these products are used for when they are recycled.
  d Try to find out where any profits from the recycling process go.

- Newspapers and magazines
- Paper
- Cardboard
- Garden waste
- Glass (clear, brown, green)
- Plastics
- Plastic bottles

B

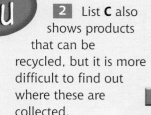

2 List **C** also shows products that can be recycled, but it is more difficult to find out where these are collected.

Try to complete activities **a–d** for these items too. You will need to do more careful research for this. You could use the following sources of information:

- local council refuse department
- supermarket chains and other shops (Sainsburys, IKEA and B & Q all have their own recycling schemes – ask Customer Services in those and other stores)
- charity shops
- internet sites.

You could start your research by using the weblink below.

3 Use all the information that you have collected to create a database for recycling in your area.

C
- Aerosols
- Building materials
- Clothes
- Electrical goods
- Furniture
- Paint
- Spectacles
- Telephone directories
- Aluminium
- Cartons
- Computer cartridges
- Foil
- Grass cuttings
- Plastic carrier bags
- Steel
- Televisions
- Batteries
- Christmas cards
- Curtains
- Food waste
- Hard core
- Rubble
- Tools – woodwork and gardening
- Used engine oil
- Books
- Christmas trees
- Drinks cans
- Fridges/freezers
- Hedge trimmings
- Soil
- Wood

4 Carry out a survey in your area, asking people these questions:

a How much do you actually recycle at present?

b Would you be willing to recycle more, if you knew where to take things?

c Would you be willing to recycle more if you knew that the profits from the recycling would go to a good cause?

d Would you be willing to recycle more if it was easy?

Then show the people you are interviewing your database, and ask them:

- How many of these recycling schemes did you know about already?
- How many of these schemes might you use now that you have this information?

5 Evaluate how successful each of the recycling schemes is. You should consider:

- how well-known the scheme is
- how accessible the collection point is
- how the scheme could be improved so that more people use it more often.

6 Choose one type of recyling that is not easily available in your neighbourhood.

a Work out a good location for a depot recycling this commodity. Remember that it must be:

- easily accessible
- secure
- in an area where it will not be a nuisance etc.

b Draw a map to show where the depot will be located.

WEBLINKS **You will find links to various sites giving information about recycling at** www.nelsonthornes.com/horizons

Where there's muck, is there brass?

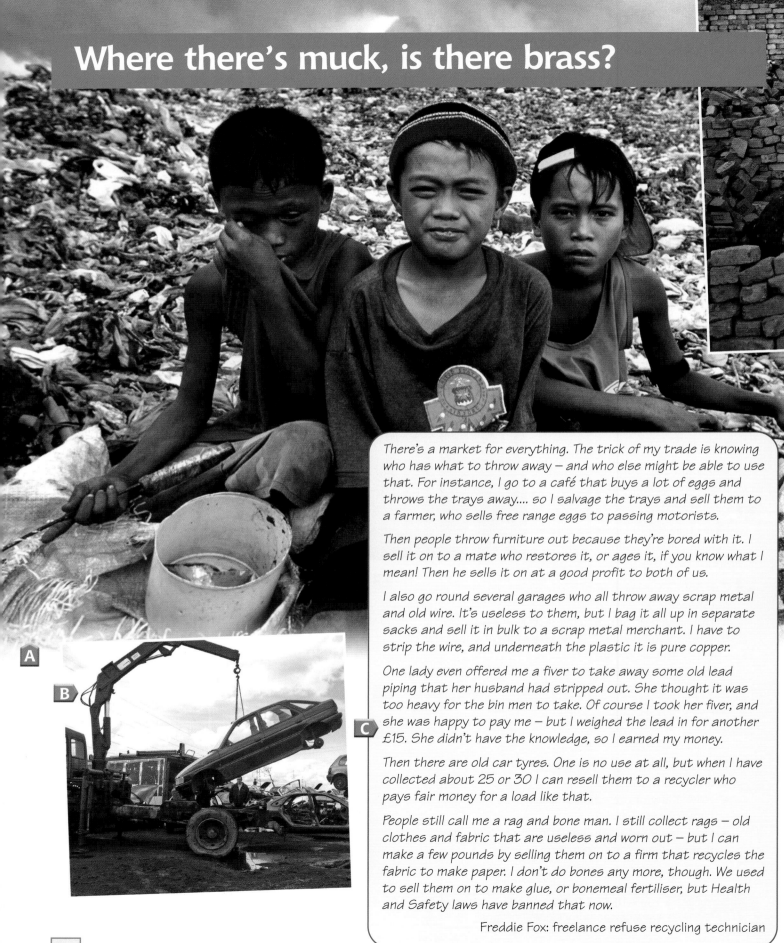

A

B

C

There's a market for everything. The trick of my trade is knowing who has what to throw away — and who else might be able to use that. For instance, I go to a café that buys a lot of eggs and throws the trays away.... so I salvage the trays and sell them to a farmer, who sells free range eggs to passing motorists.

Then people throw furniture out because they're bored with it. I sell it on to a mate who restores it, or ages it, if you know what I mean! Then he sells it on at a good profit to both of us.

I also go round several garages who all throw away scrap metal and old wire. It's useless to them, but I bag it all up in separate sacks and sell it in bulk to a scrap metal merchant. I have to strip the wire, and underneath the plastic it is pure copper.

One lady even offered me a fiver to take away some old lead piping that her husband had stripped out. She thought it was too heavy for the bin men to take. Of course I took her fiver, and she was happy to pay me — but I weighed the lead in for another £15. She didn't have the knowledge, so I earned my money.

Then there are old car tyres. One is no use at all, but when I have collected about 25 or 30 I can resell them to a recycler who pays fair money for a load like that.

People still call me a rag and bone man. I still collect rags — old clothes and fabric that are useless and worn out — but I can make a few pounds by selling them on to a firm that recycles the fabric to make paper. I don't do bones any more, though. We used to sell them on to make glue, or bonemeal fertiliser, but Health and Safety laws have banned that now.

Freddie Fox: freelance refuse recycling technician

We are from a village in Bangladesh. We do not own any land in the village. At planting time and at harvest we can get work from the big landowners, but for the rest of the year we have to travel to find work. Some of us come here to Dacca, the capital.

The lucky ones get work making bricks. That is very hard work – about 12 hours each day – carrying clay, mixing it, putting it in the moulds, emptying the finished bricks from the moulds, stacking them up, and so on.

If you don't get work there you can work outside the brickyards breaking up the bricks that were damaged during the making process. We buy these damaged bricks, using a loan from the ActionAid people. They also lend us our hammers. We have to work breaking the bricks into finer pieces.

Then we can sell them to builders and road-makers. They use the pieces in the foundations of their buildings, and for the base of the roads. They say they can work better with our fine pieces than with the rough broken bricks from the brickyards.

We earn enough money to pay off the loan and buy food. We are left with something to take home for our families when we go back to work on the farms in the village.

1 How could you reuse/recycle an old car tyre?

Try to think of at least 10 different ways.

2 Choose one of the pictures on these pages.
  a Working with a partner, write a series of questions that you would like to ask about that photo in order to find out what is happening there.
  b Swap your questions with another pair of pupils. Try to answer each other's questions. Refer to the photos and to your understanding of geography that has developed during your course.

  c The four of you should then prepare a presentation to give to the rest of the class, explaining what you have learned by 'interrogating' the photos.

3 Look carefully at all the information on these pages, and on pages 98–99. Your teacher might also give you some extra information sheets to help you.

Write two lists of points about:
  ● recycling in this country and
  ● recycling in less economically developed countries.

Are any points the same across the two lists?

4 '"Reduce, Reuse and Recycle" is essential for survival in LEDCs. It will also be essential for survival in our country.'

Write an explanation of this statement. Your answer should be planned as a response to these questions:
  ● What does 'Reduce, Reuse and Recycle' mean?
  ● Why is this essential for many poor people in LEDCs?
  ● Why does this seem less important to many people in MEDCs?
  ● Why is it becoming more important in MEDCs?
  ● In your opinion, what is the future for the 'Reduce, Reuse, Recycle' idea in this country?

OVER TO YOU

This unit has focused on you: on the resources that you use, on the footsteps that you leave on the planet, and on the way that you can reduce the size of your footprints. It should have helped you to understand the effect that you have on the planet, and why it is important to minimise your effect. In other ways it should have made you think about how sustainable your lifestyle is.

It is possible to carry out an 'environmental audit' of your life.

One simple environmental audit was produced by Christian Aid. It is a calculator to work out how much water a person, or a family, uses in a week. All the figures are averages for that use of water.

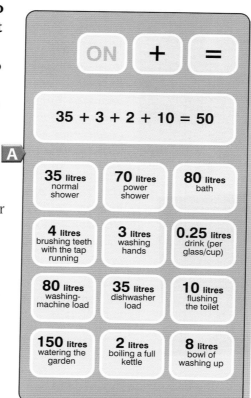

Key Words!

Audit

This is usually when a company checks the stock and the money it has. Accountants work out the value of the company, and look at the money that comes in and the money that goes out. They measure the financial health of the company.

Environmental audit

Some companies try to see how they are affecting the environment. They also try to work out how they can reduce the damage they are doing. An individual can also do an environmental audit of his or her life.

OVER TO YOU

1 a Use the Christian Aid water calculator to work out how much water you/your family use in a week.

b Ask your teacher for a checklist to see whether you are a water waster, a water watcher or a water warrior.

c Work out three things that you could do to save water. (But, as the checklist for **b** says, don't stop taking a shower, and don't suffer from dehydration. Save sensibly.)

d Share your ideas with the rest of the class. Perhaps you could take on some of each other's saving plans.

2 Audit the rubbish in your dustbin!

a Wear rubber gloves.

b Spread newspaper on the floor.

c Separate your rubbish into different piles for:
- paper
- glass
- metal
- plastic
- food
- fabrics
- others.

d Weigh each component of your rubbish.

e Tidy up!

f Present your results to show three sets:
- stuff that we do recycle
- stuff that we could recycle, but don't
- stuff that really is rubbish.

g Draw up a recycling action plan. Suggest two or three simple ideas that you can stick to. Don't suggest plans that seem magnificent but that you cannot possibly carry through.

h Share your ideas with the rest of the class. Perhaps you could take on some of each other's recycling plans.

Recycling in the future

Have you tried to reduce your footprints? If you have, well done – but individuals can only do so much. If we are to live our lives sustainably, society as a whole needs to change. Society needs to plan recycling into all its use of resources.

Statement **B** was taken from the website of a company that specialises in recycling computers and other electronic equipment.

'WEEE' is the standard laid down by the European Community for the recycling of electronic equipment. It tries to make sure that as much is reclaimed as possible. However, this is likely to be replaced in the future with laws that will require manufacturers to think about recycling as they are building products. They may have to design products so that they can be taken apart and reused or recycled when they are no longer needed.

At present, many goods are made in what are called 'assembly plants' or 'construction plants' (photo **C**). Can you imagine what the 'deconstruction' or 'disassembly plants' might be like in 'Future World'?

B

All redundant IT equipment is consigned for recycling by specialists in the secure processing of this equipment. Where practical, the equipment is refurbished and resold for reuse. If not, it is broken down to component level for reuse or, if that is not possible, broken down to the material level for raw material recovery – all in accordance with the standards laid down in WEEE.

A traditional automated construction plant – but what will deconstruction plants look like in Future World?

C

WEBLINKS **You can find out more about the company referred to above at** www.nelsonthornes.com/horizons

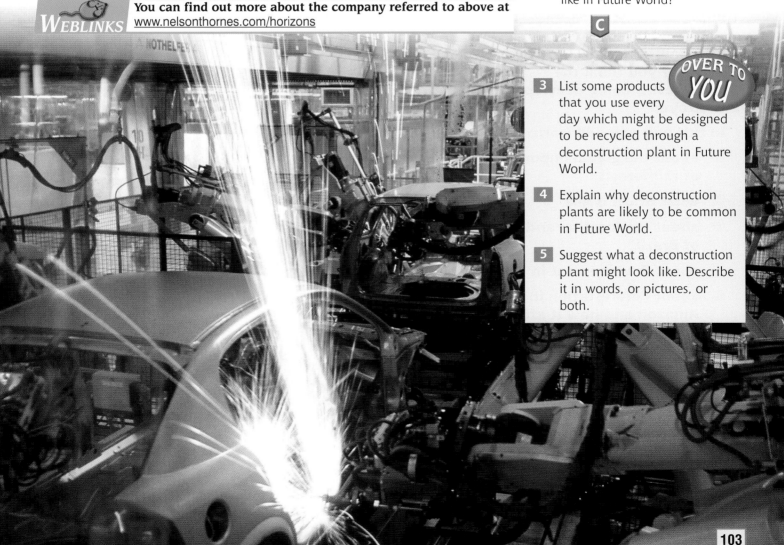

OVER TO YOU

3 List some products that you use every day which might be designed to be recycled through a deconstruction plant in Future World.

4 Explain why deconstruction plants are likely to be common in Future World.

5 Suggest what a deconstruction plant might look like. Describe it in words, or pictures, or both.

6 Development or Destruction?

Rainforests – a celebration of life

Where are we going?

The Amazon is the world's largest area of rainforest – bigger than Western Europe. If it were a country, it would be the ninth largest in the world. Much of the Amazon rainforest lies in Brazil, an LEDC that is keen to develop the potential of the region, and this often involves deforestation.

In this unit you will investigate what is happening in the Amazon from different viewpoints, and decide whether you think the rainforest is being developed or destroyed.

In this unit you will learn:

- about the global importance of rainforests

- what Brazil is like

- about the location and size of Brazil

- about development in Brazil

- about deforestation in the Amazon and how it affects different groups of people and the environment

- about sustainable development projects in the Amazon

- to conduct an enquiry using ICT, ending with a mock public debate.

Remember ...

In Unit 4 you investigated Ecosystems, and on pages 70–71 you looked at how rainforest ecosystems develop. You will need to apply your knowledge of ecosystems in this unit.

A

Emergents – the tallest trees.

Toucan

B

Undercanopy – young trees awaiting an opportunity to grow into the light.

C

The Amazon is the home of 57 endangered species, including the jaguar.

D

Large buttress roots have developed above the ground to provide support for the tall trees. The forest floor is dark and damp with little undergrowth, as sunlight is blocked by the canopy.

Fungi

Tropical rainforests are one of the wonders of nature. They are the Earth's oldest living ecosystem – Amazonia was formed between 500 million and 200 million years ago. Rainforests cover 2% of the Earth's surface, yet are home to over half its plant and animal species.

The beauty and majesty of the rainforest are indescribable. Standing in the heart of a rainforest is an awe-inspiring experience.

Canopy – a dense continous layer of trees.

Sloth

G

F

Over 300 000 species of plants have been identified, but an estimated 20 000 remain undiscovered.

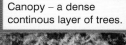

In a single hectare you might find 40 000 species of insects. They thrive in the dark, damp environment of the forest floor, playing a vital role in breaking down vegetation to form the humus layer to feed plant growth.

E

Tree frog

H

Shrub layer – at ground level where it is dark and gloomy, with little vegetation; often floods during wetter months.

OVER TO YOU

1. Why is the rainforest so important to the planet?

2. Why is the rainforest so awesome and luxuriant? *Hint:* Go back and re-read pages 70–71.

3. Imagine you are walking through a rainforest. Describe the sights and sounds and how you might feel.

4. a Conduct a search on Google for five rainforest images.
    b Insert each of your images into a PowerPoint presentation slide.
    c To each slide add a caption describing the image.
    d Join a group of four, and play back your presentations to each other.
    e Discuss which images you like the best.
    f You could print a copy of your group's favourite slides to make a display in your classroom showing your thoughts about the rainforest.

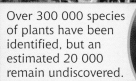

WEBLINKS **You will find a link to Google at** www.nelsonthornes.com/horizons

The rainforest covers 41% of South America. This is the Amazon rainforest – 62% lies within Brazil and the remaining 38% lies within eight surrounding countries (see satellite photo A).

The life force of the Amazon rainforest is the mighty Amazon River. It is the largest river system in the world. Its source is high in the Andes Mountains and it flows almost 6500 km across the South American continent until it enters the Atlantic Ocean at Belém in Brazil. At its mouth it is 300–500 km across, depending on the season. The Amazon river system is a major influence on the distribution of population in Brazil, as you can see on map **B**.

Amazon Rainforest
Flat, remote lowland, hot and wet climate and until recently unpenetrable rainforest

North-east coast
More reliable rainfall and fertile soil, so more suited to farming. Important ports with good harbours

North-east Brazil
Hot, dry and susceptible to drought, with thin infertile soils

Central West
Difficult for farming due to infertile soils and unreliable rainfall. Area is also remote.

South-east Brazil
Rich fertile soils and a climate well suited to farming. Plentiful supply of raw materials with well developed communication network. The main focus of industry.

A Satellite image of South America

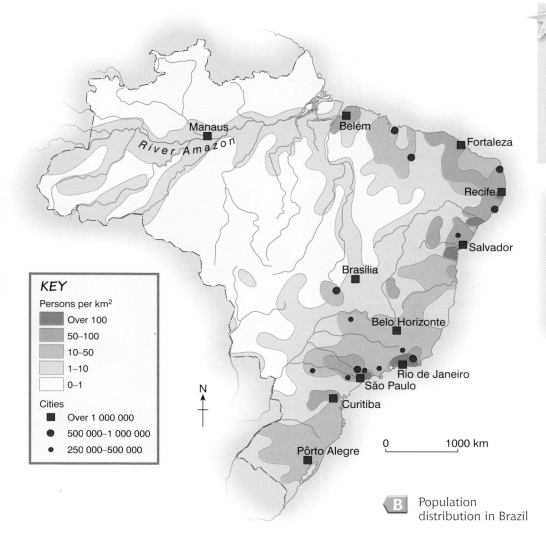

B Population distribution in Brazil

C

Brazil and Europe at the same scale

Fantastic Facts

- Brazil's total area is greater than all of Europe.
- Brazil is the fifth largest country in the world in terms of area.

OVER TO YOU

1 Compare satellite image **A** with front cover resource **B**, and name the following:
 a countries A–M
 b physical areas 1–3
 c the countries whose land area includes a part of the Amazon rainforest.

2 a Use map **A** to help you list all the countries in South America in order of size, starting with the largest.
 b The 'Fantastic Facts' and map **C** show that Brazil is larger than the whole of Europe. Use map **C** to estimate how many times larger Brazil is than the UK.

 c Use an atlas to help you list the five largest countries in the world in terms of area. Try to find out the area of each country and add it to your list.
 d Compile a second list showing the five largest countries in the world in terms of population. Why might your two lists have different countries in them?

3 Look at map **B**, showing the distribution of population in Brazil.
 a Describe the distribution shown on the map. Which parts of Brazil have the highest and lowest population density?

 b Compare maps **A** and **B** to help you explain the distribution of population in Brazil. Identify positive and negative factors from map **A**.
 c What impact does the Amazon Basin have on the distribution of population in Brazil?
 d Suggest ways that the Brazilian government could make areas with negative features more attractive for people to live in.

What is Brazil like?

You have already learned a lot about Brazil from your work so far in this unit. It is difficult to gain a true picture of what Brazil is like because it is such a large and diverse country, full of contrasts in terms of landscape, climate, people and quality of life. These images of Brazil can only provide a snapshot of this diversity.

You can find links to images and webcams of Brazil at
WEBLINKS www.nelsonthornes.com/horizons

Discuss with a partner what the images on these two pages show you about Brazil.

1 Which of the photos fit your existing knowledge of Brazil?

2 With your partner, decide which photos portray positive or negative images of Brazil.

3 a Each of you should select one of the photos that show people.
  b Identify with one of the people shown in the photo. Imagine yourself as that person for the 5 minutes leading up to the photo being taken.
  c Create a 'mind movie' of those 5 minutes, and act out your role to your partner.

4 Look back at the resources on pages 106–107 to help you match each image to a region in Brazil. Explain your choice in each case.

5 Which of the images would be used by the following people? Explain your choice in each case.
  ● An aid agency producing a leaflet to gain support for projects in Brazil
  ● A Brazilian government leaflet to attract business to the country
  ● A travel company website to attract tourists to Brazil

6 Draw a development compass rose for one of the images, and write two questions for each point on it. (Look back at pages 24–25 to remind yourself how you do this.)

7 a Search on the internet for two more photos of Brazil that provide a different image of the country. Webcams are also a useful way to get a snapshot of a place.
  b Answer the 5W questions for each photo:
    What? Where? When? Why? Who?
  c Swap photos with your partner and compare your answers.

How has Amazonia been developed?

Brazil is a rapidly developing country, although it is also one of the world's largest debtor nations. However, Brazil is much more developed than many other countries, particularly African countries such as Niger. The Brazilian government wants to develop the rainforest to help improve the quality of life of the Brazilian people.

Map **A** shows the distribution of GDP per capita for each state in Brazil. This shows that development can also be unevenly spread acoss a country, as well as across the world.

During the 1960s and 1970s the Brazilian government began to build a road network in the Amazon region. The most famous was the 5400 km Trans-Amazonian Highway (photo **B**). This was seen as the first stage of developing the region, to help move timber, crops and cattle to markets.

GDP per capita in Brazil's regions and states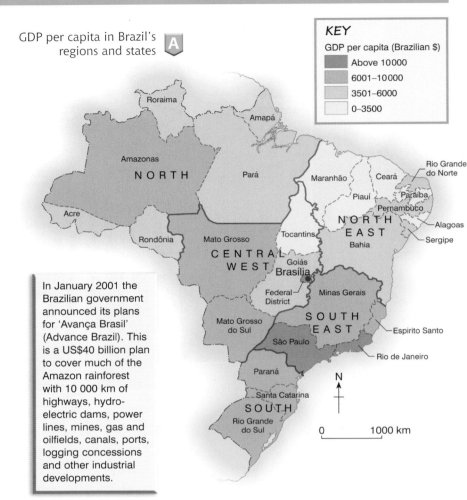

KEY
GDP per capita (Brazilian $)
- Above 10000
- 6001–10000
- 3501–6000
- 0–3500

In January 2001 the Brazilian government announced its plans for 'Avança Brasil' (Advance Brazil). This is a US$40 billion plan to cover much of the Amazon rainforest with 10 000 km of highways, hydro-electric dams, power lines, mines, gas and oilfields, canals, ports, logging concessions and other industrial developments.

Survey map of the Carajás region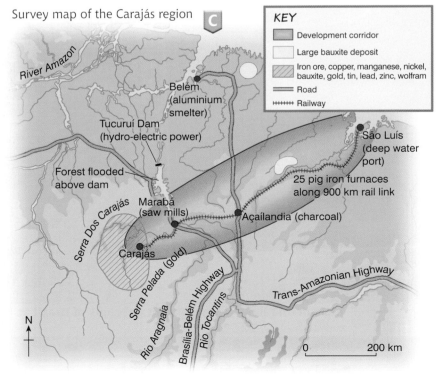

KEY
- Development corridor
- Large bauxite deposit
- Iron ore, copper, manganese, nickel, bauxite, gold, tin, lead, zinc, wolfram
- Road
- Railway

In the late 1960s the Carajás region of Pará was found to contain the biggest iron ore deposit in the world. The Grande Carajás project began in 1980, costing US$62 billion and funded with loans from MEDCs. The huge system of opencast mining operations extracts 45 million tonnes of iron ore annually, supplying industries in MEDCs. This produces export earnings and much-needed jobs for Brazil. The project has its own purpose-built power station, transport and processing plants and a 900 km rail link connecting it to port facilities and aluminium plants on the Atlantic coast at São Luís (see map **C**).

Tucuruí, the largest hydro-electric dam project in the world (photo **D**), was built to help power the Carajás Project. Completed in 1984, it has a flooded reservoir covering 4000 km² of forest. Thirty new dam projects are planned for 2010, with the potential to meet 60% of Brazil's energy needs – crucial for a country with no oil.

D Tucuruí HEP scheme

E Cattle on the former rainforest

Over 25% of the rainforest that has been cleared is now used for large-scale **cattle ranching** (photo **E**). Between 1990 and 2002, 80% of the growth in Brazil's livestock was in the Amazon region. Much of the beef produced is exported to MEDCs.

One of the most valuable resources in the rainforest are the trees themselves (photo **F**). Tropical hardwoods, such as mahogany, are much sought after. **Logging** is a major activity within the Amazon.

F

OVER TO YOU

1. a Use the resources in Unit 2 '80:20' pages 26–29 to determine how developed Brazil is. (You could find out which GDP band Brazil is in from map **A** on pages 26–27, and its Human Development Index from map **C** on page 29.)
   b Look back at your enquiry work for Unit 2, on pages 30–31. Look at the development data for the countries shown on spreadsheet **A**.
   c How developed is Brazil compared with the other countries in the spreadsheet?

2. a Look at map **A**. Which regions of Brazil appear to be:
   - the most developed
   - the least developed?

   b Use satellite image **A** and map **B** on pages 106–107 to try to explain the uneven distribution of wealth in Brazil.

3. Brazilian politicians coined a slogan when Amazonia was first being opened up:
   'Land without people. For people without land.'
   Explain what they meant by this slogan.

4. What are the advantages for developing hydro-electric power stations in the Amazon rainforest?

5. Write a 100-word summary explaining the benefits of these development projects for Brazil.

What is life like for tribal people?

Most Amazon tribes live by a mixture of hunting, gathering and growing crops. Each tribe is unique, with its own culture, mythology, beliefs, art and rituals. Many ecologists and environmentalists believe that *indigenous (native) people* can teach us a lot about sustainable living.

The Yanomami (which means 'human beings') are the largest tribe in the Amazon to have kept their traditional way of life. Their territory covers an area of approximately 192 000 km², located on both sides of the border between Brazil and Venezuela.

Some users of the rainforest are not sensitive to the needs of tribal people. During the 1970s and 1980s, Brazilian goldminers invaded the land of the Yanomami. This destroyed their villages and exposed the Yanomami to diseases to which they had no immunity. As a result, 20% of the tribe died in just seven years.

The Yanomami do not have proper ownership rights over their land – Brazil refuses to recognise tribal land ownership. Many tribes are moved when land is flooded for the construction of HEP schemes. Tribes are beginning to fight to protect their lands, forests and traditions. A fight that began with weapons has evolved into a war of words. Chief Raoni, of the Kayapo Nation, went to the Brazilian capital to explain to the government how their environment was being destroyed.

The Yanomami live in small independent village groups. The area of forest used by each Yanomami house-village can be described as a series of concentric circles, each used for a specific purpose, as shown in diagram **A**.

Each local Yanomami group lives in a communal house called a **shabono**. It is a huge doughnut-shaped structure, up to 40 metres across, made of logs and thatching, with a central open courtyard for dancing and ceremonies. Each family has its own hearth under the covered edge of the building, where they sleep in hammocks around their fire.

This area is for the collective expeditions, lasting one to two weeks, to hunt for the abundant game in the area. Hunters are afraid of vengeful spirits in their prey, so they are careful not to hunt more game than they need. In this way, the long-term survival of wildlife in the forest is assured.

10–20 km radius

A

- Amazonian tribes speak at least 170 different languages and dialects.

5–10 km radius

5 km radius

This area is used by the community for living and farming, with females gathering crops, and occasional brief hunting trips.

The shabono is always near running water and vegetable gardens. Crop cultivation accounts for 80% of the group's food, mainly banana and plantain trees. Over 60% of crops are used for medicine, religious ceremonies, tools and household goods. Amazonian soil is not very fertile, so a new garden is cleared every two or three years. Land is left for 10–50 years before it is farmed again. This type of farming is called **shifting cultivation**.

Individual hunting (*rama huu*) and day-to-day family food gathering.

C

Hunting, gathering and fishing account for 20% of the Yanomami's food. Gathering wild nuts and fruit is women's work. The rainforest provides the Yanomami with an excellent diet.

OVER TO YOU

1
a Who are the Yanomami and where do they live?
b Describe their way of life.

2 Write a list of the different ways tribal people use forest resources.

3 How has the lifestyle of tribal people changed as the Amazon has been developed?

4 Why is it important that we learn from such tribes?

5 In Unit 5 you investigated your 'global footprint'.
a Compare the size of *your* global footprint with that of the Yanomami – whose is the smallest?
b Do you or the Yanomami live a more sustainable lifestyle?

6 Imagine you are a graphic designer and you have won a contract from Survival International, an organisation committed to campaigning on behalf of tribal groups around the world. You are to design a poster for a new campaign to promote the lifestyle of tribal people in the Amazon.

Comment on each other's posters as you did in Unit 5.

WEBLINKS You will find a link to Survival International, and to another website giving information and photos of tribal people in the Amazon to help with your poster, at www.nelsonthornes.com/horizons

Why do people live in the rainforest?

Many people have migrated to the Amazon from different parts of Brazil, attracted by the frontier spirit and perceived opportunities for a better quality of life.

Landless peasants and settlers have followed the logging companies along the roads into untouched rainforest lands, burning off whatever was left behind.

Between 1995 and 1998 the Brazilian government granted land in the Amazon to roughly 150 000 families. Poor farmers chop down a small area (usually only a few hectares) and burn the tree trunks – a process called 'slash and burn'. These are subsistence farmers who mainly grow just enough crops to feed the family. Forest trees are cut and the area is left to dry for a few months and then burnt. The land is planted with crops like bananas, palms, manioc, maize or rice. After a year or two, the productivity of the soil declines, and the farmers clear new areas of forest for cultivation. The old, infertile land is used for cattle grazing or left.

Key Words!

Rubber/latex

The **rubber** tree (*hevea brasiliensis*) is native to the Amazon rainforests, growing to over 30 metres tall. These trees are tapped for their **latex** (from which rubber is made), which is produced in their bark. A rubber tapper is a forest worker who 'taps' rubber trees, extracting the latex.

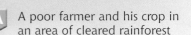

A A poor farmer and his crop in an area of cleared rainforest

> I've come to the rainforest from Pernambuco in the north-east of Brazil, where I was a 50–50 **sharecropper** growing sugar cane – 50% of what I earned went to the landowner. There was regular drought and my crops were destroyed. I had no money or future there. Then I heard that the government would give me my own land and a house in the Amazon. I jumped at the chance to get a decent life for me and my family. I now have my own land to farm, although we're frightened of the tribal people who sometimes attack us. My small plot of land doesn't make much difference – the rainforest is so huge.

 A rubber tapper

I walk along trails containing up to 200 rubber trees. At each tree I make a diagonal cut in the bark to make the latex run into a small metal cup that I place at the end of the cut. I return later to each tree to pick up the latex that has collected in the tins. On the trail I also collect Brazil nuts, which I can sell. It's back-breaking work – the cutting and collecting can take me up to 10 hours.

I spend a further 2 hours processing the rubber into a ball for sale. I don't earn a lot. Life has become more difficult since the government encouraged people from the south of Brazil to buy land here. They want to clear forest for cattle ranching. They've tried to move us off the land, sometimes resorting to violence.

The **rubber** boom started in Brazil at the beginning of the 1900s. The Amazon was at first the only source of rubber, until seeds were smuggled out of Brazil. The rubber tappers were mostly poor Brazilians from the north-east. In Brazil, trees are left in their natural environment, the rainforest, and paths are cut into the forest to connect them. Rubber tappers work in the states of Amazonas, Rondônia and Acre.

Amazonian rubber is insignificant in the world economy today – production is approximately 25 000 tonnes annually, compared with Malaysia's 1.7 million tonnes. Here, rubber trees are grown in **plantations** so that it is much easier to collect the **latex** as all the trees are together.

OVER TO YOU

Photos **A** and **B** show two people who have moved into the rainforest in search of a better quality of life.

1 Working with a partner, imagine you had a webcam link with the poor farmer and the rubber tapper. Write a series of questions you would like to ask them about their life and what they feel about the rainforest.
   a Swap your questions with another pair in your class, and attempt to answer each other's questions.
   b Write a summary of your findings, outlining the lifestyle of each.

2 Why did poor farmers move to the rainforest?

3 Why do you think the rubber industry of Brazil is so small compared with that of Malaysia?

4 Look at back cover resource **D**. Select the two different areas where you think the rubber tappers and poor farmers are likely to live. In each case explain your choice, using evidence from the satellite image.

5 Both the rubber tapper and the poor farmer conflict with other users of the rainforest. Identify who they are in conflict with and explain why there is a problem.

Is the rainforest being destroyed?

In less than 50 years, more than half of the world's tropical rainforests have been lost to fire and the chainsaw, and the rate of destruction is still accelerating. In 2000 alone, almost 2 million hectares of rainforest in the Brazilian Amazon were destroyed for logging, mining, industry, farming and road building. Around 15% of the Amazon rainforest has already been destroyed. A significant part of what remains is under direct threat – as are the forest plants, the animals and the people who depend on the forest.

Causes of deforestation

There is no one cause of **deforestation**. The Brazilian government plans for 'Avança Brasil' (see page 110) will lead to massive destruction of rainforest. HEP schemes flood vast areas of forest. New roads open up more of the forest for people to clear. Rich landowners in Brazil slash and burn huge tracts of land in the rainforest. They seed it with grass for cattle ranching, and earn millions of dollars in government-subsidised loans in return for developing the land.

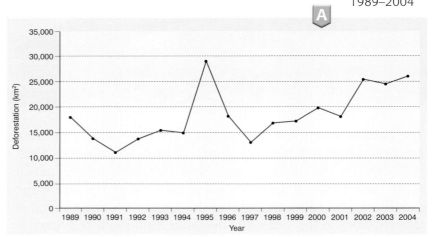

Deforestation in Brazil, 1989–2004

A

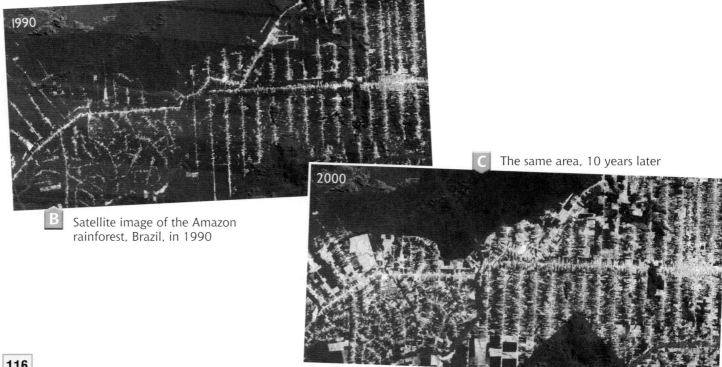

1990

B Satellite image of the Amazon rainforest, Brazil, in 1990

C The same area, 10 years later

2000

However, the Brazilian government is not the only cause of deforestation. Illegal logging accounts for around 80% of all timber produced in the Brazilian Amazon. Countries such as the USA, Italy, France, the UK and Japan do not monitor closely the source of the timber they import. Poor landless farmers use fire for clearing land.

Soyabeans have recently become a major contributor to deforestation. A new variety of soyabean has been developed by Brazilian scientists to flourish in the rainforest climate. Brazil is on the verge of overtaking the USA as the world's leading exporter of soyabeans.

Environmental groups

Many environmental groups are campaigning to pressurise world governments, in particular the Brazilian government, to stop deforestation and protect the remaining rainforest before it is too late. Screenshot **D** shows the campaign website of one of the many environmental groups, Rainforest Action Network (RAN).

WEBLINKS **You will find links to the Amazon monitoring site and to RAN at** www.nelsonthornes.com/horizons

---

1 What is deforestation?

2 Look at graph **A**.
  a What is it showing about the rates of deforestation in Brazil?
  b When did deforestation reach its peak?
  c What area was deforested in that year?
  d Does the graph suggest that deforestation levels are now likely to decline?

3 The two satellite images **B** and **C** show the same area of rainforest over 10 years.
  a How has this area changed?
  b What new developments can you identify on the images?

c The Brazilian government has developed its own satellite image system for the Amazon to monitor levels of deforestation. It can be viewed on the internet. Go to the website and find out about current levels of destruction.

4 a Go to the RAN website.
  b In which country is this environmental action group based?
  c What is the mission statement for RAN?
  d Why is it campaigning to protect the rainforest?

5 a What are the main causes of deforestation in the Amazon?
  b For each cause you identify, give a reason to explain how it contributes to deforestation.
  c Which do you think is the most important cause of deforestation?

6 a What viewpoint is cartoon **E** portraying about logging?
  b Why is the text in Portuguese?
  c Draw your own cartoon to portray a different cause of deforestation in the Amazon.

OVER TO YOU

What are the consequences of deforestation?

The rainforest ecosystem has taken millions of years to evolve and is very fragile. The diversity of life in the rainforest is important to all of us. Deforestation has major consequences at local and global scales. Photo A shows how deforestation affects the ecosystem at a local level.

Remember ...

You learned on pages 70–71 how the rainforest ecosystem worked.

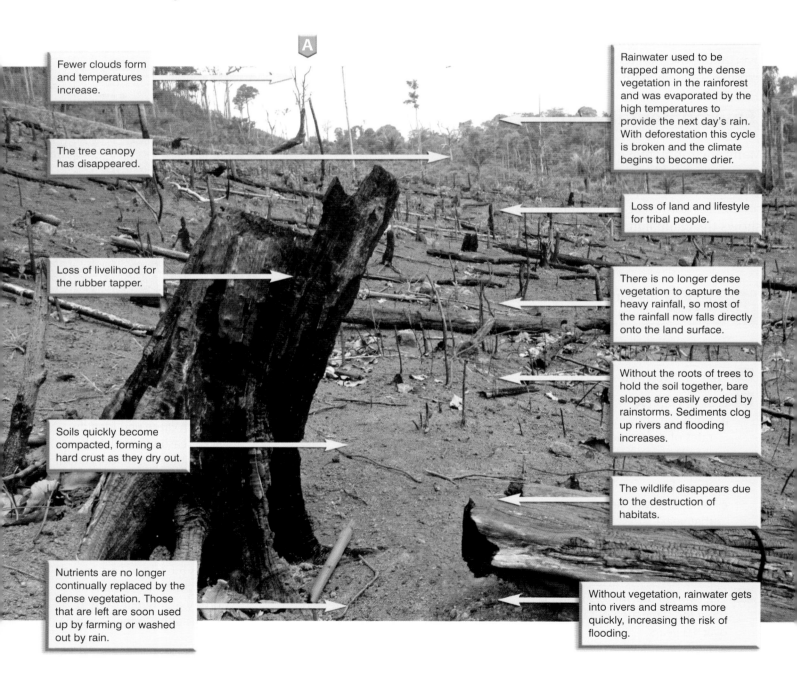

A

Fewer clouds form and temperatures increase.

The tree canopy has disappeared.

Loss of livelihood for the rubber tapper.

Soils quickly become compacted, forming a hard crust as they dry out.

Nutrients are no longer continually replaced by the dense vegetation. Those that are left are soon used up by farming or washed out by rain.

Rainwater used to be trapped among the dense vegetation in the rainforest and was evaporated by the high temperatures to provide the next day's rain. With deforestation this cycle is broken and the climate begins to become drier.

Loss of land and lifestyle for tribal people.

There is no longer dense vegetation to capture the heavy rainfall, so most of the rainfall now falls directly onto the land surface.

Without the roots of trees to hold the soil together, bare slopes are easily eroded by rainstorms. Sediments clog up rivers and flooding increases.

The wildlife disappears due to the destruction of habitats.

Without vegetation, rainwater gets into rivers and streams more quickly, increasing the risk of flooding.

Global consequences

Deforestation of the Amazon has global consequences. It is estimated that the planet is losing 137 plant, animal and insect species every single day due to deforestation – that's 50 000 species a year. Rainforests currently provide the source for 25% of today's medicines – 70% of the plants with anti-cancer properties are found only in the rainforest. The forests could hold the key to curing many major diseases in the future.

In Brazil alone, more than 90 native tribes have been wiped out in the last century, and with them their knowledge of the medicinal value of rainforest species. Many of the foods we eat today originated in rainforests: avocado, banana, black pepper, Brazil nuts, cinnamon, coffee and vanilla.

Rainforests play a critical role in the atmosphere because they hold vast reserves of carbon in their vegetation. When rainforests are burnt, or trees are cut and left to decay, the carbon is released into the atmosphere as carbon dioxide (CO_2). Scientists estimate that Brazil's carbon emissions may have risen by as much as 50% since 1990, making it one of the 10 top polluters in the world.

The rainforest is a fragile ecosystem that can be affected by changes in human activity and climate change. Scientific research conducted jointly by Brazil and international organisations, such as the UK Meteorological Office, concluded that the Amazon forest will perish if the current trend in global climate change is not reversed. The global reduction in carbon emissions is a necessary condition for the survival of the rainforest. Developed countries have a major responsibility for this.

President of Brazil, Luiz Inacio Lula da Silva **B**

Links to... Your investigation of global warming in Unit 5 pages 86–91 links to the consequences of deforestation.

OVER TO YOU

1 Look back at Unit 4 'Ecosystems' pages 70–71. These pages explained how the rainforest ecosystem works, using mind maps. Create your own mind map to show the consequences of deforestation on the rainforest ecosystem, using photo **A** on page 118 to help you.

2 Explain why deforestation:
   a makes soils less fertile
   b makes flooding more frequent.

3 Look at photo **A** and compare it with other photos of the rainforest in this unit. Describe what the feelings of the following people might be towards the forest before and after it has been chopped down.
   ● You
   ● A rubber tapper
   ● A logger

4 Why is deforestation of the rainforest an important global issue?

5 Read speech bubble **B** carefully. The Brazilian President is suggesting that developed countries are also contributing to the problems of the Amazon rainforest.
   a Explain how the Brazilian government thinks developed countries are affecting the rainforest.
   b Look back at pages 110–111 and 116–117 and identify other ways that developed countries have contributed to deforestation in the Amazon.

6

You from the developed world are all in Brazil to stop us exploiting the wealth of the Amazon. What arrogance! You've already destroyed all the forests in your own nations and so you come and lecture us about the environment!

This is another Brazilian point of view. Do you think it is fair that developed countries try to stop countries such as Brazil from developing the rainforest? (Think about your findings from question 5.)

Can the rainforest be developed sustainably?

Look back at Unit 2 '80:20' pages 40–41. There you investigated the meaning of sustainable development. Cutting down rainforest and changing the ecosystem for ever is clearly unsustainable. There are a number of sustainable development projects taking place in the Amazon rainforest. You have already investigated some of these.

> **Remember ...**
>
> Re-read pages 40–41 to remind yourself about sustainable development.

Scientists now agree that by leaving the rainforests intact and harvesting their many natural resources they have more economic value than if they were cut down for timber or for grazing cattle. Research shows that rainforest land converted to cattle operations yields $150 per hectare each year, and if timber is harvested the land yields $988 per hectare. However, if renewable and sustainable resources such as nuts, fruit and medicinal plants are harvested, the land yields $5930 per hectare. This provides an income not only today but for generations to come, while still protecting the forest and giving employment to local inhabitants.

Many sustainable projects are needed to protect the Amazon rainforest and its resources. To be effective, they must maintain people's quality of life and ensure the long-term protection of the forest and its unique plants and animals. These goals can only be achieved if sound environmental and economic alternatives replace the current destructive approaches.

Today, local people can earn 5–10 times more by harvesting medicinal plants, fruits, nuts and oils than by chopping down the forest for subsistence. Resources **A**–**C** provide examples of sustainable projects currently being developed in the Amazon rainforest.

Ecotourism is a sustainable use of the rainforests. Visitors to tropical rainforest areas stay in environmentally friendly accommodation and learn about the forests from the local community. This provides income to support conservation. Tourists could become future conservation campaigners once they appreciate the beauty and value of the rainforest.

> *We respect nature and, by including qualified local labour into our operations, even where this would not be necessary, we also help to improve social conditions in the areas we visit.*

A

Remember ...

You investigated ecotourism in *Horizons 2* pages 120–121.

B

Brazil Creates Largest Rainforest Reserve

Friday, 23 August 2002

The government of Brazil has announced the creation of the largest tropical forest reserve in the world, in collaboration with environmental groups such as WWF. The Tumucumaque National Park, in the northern Amazonian state of Amapa, will cover 3 870 000 hectares – an area the size of Switzerland. The reserve is thought to contain many unidentified plants and unique animal species. Access to the park is quite difficult: local rivers are impossible to navigate for most of the year, and there are no roads. As a result, Tumucumaque is one of only a few forests still unaltered by humans. 'Plants and animals that may be endangered elsewhere will continue to thrive in our forests forever,' said Dr Claude Martin, Director General of WWF International. 'It is a significant first step to achieve the strict protection of at least 10 per cent of the Amazon forests in Brazil.'

From BBC News at bbcnews.com

C

Raintree Nutrition, Incorporated was founded in 1995.

The company advocates the preservation of rainforests by promoting the use and creating consumer markets for sustainable and renewable rainforest resources and products, with special emphasis on its important medicinal plants.

We export worldwide over 60 sustainable rainforest plants, resins and oils from the Amazon; developing over 60 rainforest herbal formulas and extracts.

Most of our products are harvested by the indigenous tribal people of the rainforest.

Find out more at
Raintree Nutrition, Inc.
Carson City, Nevada USA
Website: www.RaintreeNutrition.com

OVER TO YOU

1 a Look back at pages 110–119 and consider all the human activities in the rainforest.
  b Draw a two-column table, headed Sustainable and Unsustainable.
  c Write each human activity in the rainforest in the appropriate column.

2 a Make another copy of diagram **I** on page 41.
  b Label each section of the diagram to show the social, economic and environmental factors that need to be considered in sustainable development projects in the rainforest.

3 How can sustainable development projects help protect rainforests?

4 a What is ecotourism?
  b Identify the attractions of holidays in the rainforest from screenshot **A**.

5 Explain how the schemes shown in resources **A**, **B** and **C** are examples of sustainable development.

6 Do you think each of these schemes will help Brazil to become more developed? Explain your answer.

In this unit you have learned:

- about the global importance of rainforests
- what Brazil is like
- about the location and size of Brazil
- about development in Brazil
- about deforestation in the Amazon and how it affects different groups of people and the environment
- about sustainable development projects in the Amazon.

You are going to apply your knowledge and understanding of this unit to an enquiry debate in the form of a mock public meeting. Your class will be divided into 4 groups. Each group will represent the views of one of the groups of people shown in resource **A** to discuss the key question: Amazonia – development or destruction?

The rainforest debate **A**

Tribal people

Poor farmer

Amazonia – Development or Destruction?

Brazilian government

Environmentalists

Step 1

Preparing the investigation

1 Re-read the section of this unit that tells you about the point of view you will be presenting in the debate.

2 In your group, think of additional key questions that will help you represent this point of view.

3 Your group will need to agree on a slogan, or *mission statement*, that will summarise the view of the group of people you are representing.

Step 2

Collecting information

4 Your teacher will provide you with some basic information about the group you are representing, but you will also need to do some research on the internet. You should use a search engine to look for websites that present particular points of view.

WEBLINKS **You will find links to sites presenting the views of your group of people and the Google search engine at** www.nelsonthornes.com/horizons

 Step 3

Presenting your findings

5 Each group will produce a presentation for the mock public meeting, to last for no more than 10 minutes. Members of your group should take responsibility for different activities as follows:
- Use desktop publishing software to create a brochure and posters promoting your viewpoint – include images, logos and quotes from your internet research.
- Use PowerPoint to create your presentation – again, include the resources from your internet research.
- Use a spreadsheet to create charts for any statistics you have found that back up your viewpoint. These charts can also be used in the brochure, PowerPoint presentation, posters and display.
- Create a classroom display, ideally in the room where the debate will take place – include a banner, your group's brochure, posters and slides from the PowerPoint presentation.
- Use a video camera to make a short video presentation supporting your viewpoint.

Tips for your presentation
- Try to include your group's agreed key questions and slogan in all of the materials you produce.
- Your group should meet to check on progress and to ensure that the activities fit together.
- You will need to rehearse the presentation with everyone in the group.
- You will have to work to a deadline – your teacher will tell you when your group's presentation will take place.

6 **a** Set up the classroom as a public meeting room, with an area for each group.
b Each group should sit in their area, in front of their own display.
c Your group could dress up in character.
d Before your group's presentation, give everyone in the class a copy of your brochure.
e Each group then makes a 10-minute presentation to the rest of the class. Each member of your group should be involved. Use your PowerPoint presentation as a guide and make reference to your brochure and display.

 Step 4

Analysing the results

7 When all the presentations have been made, hold a class debate on the motion:
'Is the Amazon rainforest being developed or destroyed?'
You should remain in character while taking part in the debate.

 Step 5

Reaching a conclusion

8 At the end of the debate, vote on the motion, ideally in character. If each of the groups has presented their views well, your vote might not be as straightforward as you thought!

9 Produce a piece of extended writing summarising the views presented in the meeting. Add a conclusion giving your own views on what is happening in the rainforest, and what should happen in the future.

 Step 6

Evaluating your work

10 Once you have finished your writing, share your own views about the rainforest with a partner.

11 Why is it important to approach websites on the internet critically and to consider the motives of the information providers?

PASSPORT TO THE WORLD

Why continue your studies in Geography?

You've made it and reached the end of *Horizons*. Well done! We hope you have enjoyed the journey and that what you have learned has helped you to become better geographers. If you have enjoyed Geography, you may be thinking of carrying on to study it in Years 10 and 11 and maybe at A level. Geography is a popular subject at GCSE and A level.

The geographical skills, knowledge and understanding that you have developed with *Horizons* are useful in a wide variety of careers. Let's meet three people who studied geography and now have successful careers ...

Ruth travelled the world – here she is at Fox Glacier in New Zealand

My name is Ruth. I'm 24 years old and I'm currently a Graduate Trainee with Wigan Council. As part of the graduate training scheme I've worked in the Planning and Regeneration Department and the Department of Engineering Services, where my knowledge of both physical and human geography has been of great value to my work.

When I was at High School I studied GCSE Geography, which I really enjoyed. So I decided to study it at A level as well. I think Geography is a really interesting subject – you learn about things that have shaped our world and that affect everybody, every day of our lives.

I didn't study Geography at university, but after I graduated I decided to continue my interest in Geography by spending 6 months travelling around the world. I had a fantastic time, saw some amazing sights and met loads of brilliant people. I feel that having an understanding and appreciation of our environment and the world we live in helped to make my experience even more fulfilling.

Alan at Wadi Rum Spring

My name is Alan. I'm a freelance journalist, consultant and researcher, specialising in the politics and economy of the Middle East.

I studied Geography at school and passed O and A level. I became very interested in travel and exploration, so after travelling around the Middle East for 6 months I went to university to study Geography. I went on to do an MA in the Geography of the Middle East, and then did my PhD on aspects of tourism geography in Syria.

I moved into journalism, and have written regularly for the Observer, the Guardian and the Evening Standard, and for papers and magazines in Italy, Austria, France, Norway and Saudi Arabia. I also broadcast on TV and radio in the UK, Europe and the USA, and have written two books.

I have homes in London and Barcelona. London is where the work is and Barcelona is where I go to relax. It's also a good base for my travels in the Middle East. I go there as often as possible – remember, it was travel that turned me on to Geography in the first place!

Clare, in India

Geography has always been my passion and I've used it for work and pleasure. After leaving school, I went to the University of Hull to study Geography. I went on to the University of Sheffield to do an MA in Town and Regional Planning.

Since 1998 I've worked on community regeneration, initially in Sheffield and now in Doncaster with the New Deal for Communities (NDC) programme. NDC looks at the root causes of deprivation, leading to long-term sustainable improvements in the standard of living of the local community. The great thing about the job is that it's geography in action. We work with the community to plan their own environment, empowering them to deal with the issues that affect their quality of life.

I've been lucky enough to travel and experience many different cultures and environments. Wherever you are, geography is all around you. The more places I go to and the more people I meet, the more new things about geography I learn.

1 How has geography influenced the lives of Ruth, Alan and Clare?

2 Throughout the *Horizons* series we have included Passport to the World boxes in most units. These should have given you an insight into how Geography is useful for a wide range of careers. Go back through *Horizons 1–3*, find all these Passport to the World boxes and compile a list of all the different careers that are linked to Geography.

What have you enjoyed most about the Horizons geography course? Do you think this could influence your choice of subjects next year?

You can find out more about Geography at GCSE and A level, as well as careers using Geography, from your Geography teacher, school careers adviser, and on the internet.

WEBLINKS **You can find more about careers using Geography at** www.nelsonthornes.com/horizons

Glossary

Page numbers in *italics* indicate the first main reference in the text (no page numbers for 'How to' words). Each geographical term is colour coded by unit.

'How to' words

Analyse Look at this in great detail. Try to see what has caused this place or thing to be like it is.

Annotate Add notes around the map or sketch to explain the geography.

Classify Organise into groups and sub-groups. All items in a group have something in common.

Compare Look at two places together. Show how they are similar and how they are different.

Conclude Make a final point to sum up what you think.

Critically evaluate To test the reliability of information and findings.

Describe Say what you can see here (or what you can hear, touch, etc.)

Enquire Find out all about.

Evaluate Say how well something has been done. What were its strengths and weaknesses?

Explain Give reasons for something.

Identify Say what this is.

Interpret Look carefully at something, then say what it means.

Investigate Look into something very carefully and find out all about it.

Justify When you have made a statement, give your reasons for it.

Suggest You may not be sure what the answer is – but make a sensible suggestion.

Summarise Write a brief summing-up of something, giving the main points.

Geographical words and terms

A

Active volcano A volcano that has erupted in living memory. *13*

Aftershock Another earthquake that follows after a major quake. These can do serious damage to buildings weakened by the first shock. *9*

Andesite Thicker, sticky lava that often produces explosive eruptions with clouds of ash. *14*

Audit When a company checks the stock and money that it has. *102*

B

Basalt Hot, runny lava that cools into fine-grained, dark rock. *14*

Bilateral aid Aid that is given, or lent, from the government of one country to the government of another country. *21*

C

Canopy The upper layer of the rainforest, where the trees' branches tangle together as they try to reach the sunlight. *70*

Cattle ranching Keeping large numbers of cattle in a large open space. The cattle roam freely and are then rounded up for fattening up for meat. *111*

Collision zone The place where two plates collide and the surface is forced up to form fold mountain ranges. *7*

Constructive margin Where plates pull apart from each other and new crust is made. *7*

Consume To eat, but also to use up resources in other ways such as using fuel, using up space, making use of people's services, etc. *84*

Convection current Movements in the semi-molten rocks of the upper mantle, caused by rising currents of hot rock. *7*

Core The dense inner part of the Earth. Made of iron and nickel, it has an outer core that is liquid and an inner core that is solid. *7*

Creep metre Measures any movements in the land surface and may show when the sides of a volcano are starting to slip, just before an eruption. *18*

Crumb Particles of soil, made when minerals and humus bond together. *68*

Crust The solid outer layer of the Earth's rocks. It is between 6 and 70 km thick. *7*

Deforestation The clearance of forested areas by people, causing permanent damage to the ecosystem. *117*

D

Destructive margin Where plates crash into each other and crust is destroyed. *7*

Dormant volcano A volcano that is 'asleep' but has erupted during recorded history and may erupt again. *13*

E

Earth Summit A meeting of the world's countries in 1992 which agreed on a plan for sustainable development. *40*

Ecosystem A community of plants and animals (including people) and the climate and soils that interact with them. *64*

Ecotourism A sustainable form of tourism. Visitors come to enjoy the natural environment of an area. They do as little damage as possible to the natural environment and indigenous people. *120*

Emergency relief Money, supplies and services that are sent to an area just after it has suffered a disaster. *21*

Environmental audit When a company or individual works out how they are affecting (damaging or conserving) the environment. *102*

Epicentre The point on the Earth's surface directly above the focus (the place where the earthquake happened). *9*

Extinct volcano A volcano that has erupted in the past but will not erupt again. *13*

F

Fairtrade Fairtrade is a system of trading that makes sure that small, independent farmers in poor countries get a reasonable price for the crops that they grow. *38*

Farmers' market A market where farmers and growers from an area are present in person to sell their own produce direct to the public. *93*

Fauna The animals that live in an ecosystem. *71*

Fossil fuels Fuels that come from the remains of plants and animals, stored in the rock below ground. Includes coal, oil and natural gas. Non-renewable. *88*

G

Global positioning satellite (GPS) A satellite that provides information and feedback to trackers on the Earth. They can be used to work out precise positions on the Earth's surface. *18*

Gross Domestic Product (GDP) The value of all the goods and services produced in a nation in any one year. It is often divided by the number of people in the country to give GDP/person. *26*

H

Horizon A layer in the soil. The A horizon is near the surface and contains mainly organic matter. The C horizon consists of broken mineral material. The B horizon is a mixed layer. **68**

Human Development Index (HDI) Measures development by combining measures of life expectancy, education and income/capita. Has a value between 0 (low) and 1 (high). **29**

Humus Decayed plant and animal material that forms part of the soil. **68**

I

Indigenous (native) people The original inhabitants of an area who lived there before outside settlers moved in. **112**

Input Something that comes into a system from the outside. Water, organic matter and broken rock are the main inputs into soil. **69**

Intensity The measure of the effects of an earthquake. **9**

L

Laser reflector Lasers rays are sent out and reflected back again. The time taken can be measured to give a precise record of distance travelled. **18**

Latex The sap of the rubber tree that is the raw material for making rubber. **115**

Lava Molten rock that has reached the surface of the Earth. **13**

LEDC A less economically developed country. It is important to remember that some LEDCs have highly developed culture, art, religious belief system, etc. They are not just 'less developed'. **27**

Liana A tall, thin plant that winds around trees and uses them as support to reach up to the canopy for sunlight. **70**

Liquefaction The process in an earthquake when the movement of the energy waves causes the ground to act like a liquid. **9**

Logging Cutting down trees for wood or to make wood pulp, a raw material for paper. **111**

M

Magma Molten rock still below the Earth's surface. **13**

Magnitude The measure of how much energy is released by an earthquake. **9**

Mantle The layer of the Earth between the core and the crust. It is semi-molten and can flow slowly. **7**

Maquiladora A Mexican assembly plant for manufactured goods of all sorts. **56**

MEDC A more economically developed country. **27**

Minerals Fragments of broken rock that form part of the soil. **68**

Multilateral aid Aid that is given, or lent, from MEDCs to LEDCs through a multinational organisation like the World Bank or the International Monetary Fund. **21**

N

Natural hazard A hazard is a threat to people or the environment. A natural hazard is caused by earth movements or the weather. **5**

Nomad A person who moves from place to place with no fixed home. They often live in areas with different seasons and move to find new pastures. **78**

North–South line The Brandy Report in 1980 saw that the world was divided between the more developed North and the less developed South. **27**

O

Overpopulated Places where the total population cannot be supported by the area's resources, given their level of technical development. **50**

P

Pastoral farming Keeping animals for meat, milk, hides, etc. **79**

Plantation A large area set aside for the commercial production of crops, usually trees. **115**

Plate tectonics The idea that the Earth's surface is divided into a number of plates that move slowly across the globe. **5**

Population density The number of people who live on an area of land, usually measured in persons/km^2. **48**

Prairie lands Grasslands in the central areas of the USA and Canada. **54**

R

Remote sensing Using satellite images to find out about the surface of the Earth. **18**

Rhyolite Very sticky lava that can produce explosive, destructive eruptions. **14**

Richter scale The scale that gives the magnitude of an earthquake. Below 3 can be felt only by a seismometer. Above 5 can cause serious damage to buildings. **9**

Rubber Rubber originally came from the sap (or latex) of the rubber tree. Now, much rubber is synthetic (i.e. it is made chemically from petroleum). **115**

S

Seismometer An instrument that measures the shaking of the ground during an earthquake. **9**

Shabono The large communal hut that is home to a whole group of Yanomani in Brazil's rainforest. **112**

Sharecropper A poor farmer who is loaned farmland by a rich landowner. Half of the profits have to be paid to the landowner each year. **114**

Slash-and-burn cultivation The system of farming where new land is used every few years. Vegetation is cut down, left to dry, then burnt off to create new farmland. **52**

Slip (or passive) margin Where plates slide past each other and crust is neither made nor destroyed. **7**

Staple food Food that provides people with their main energy supply. They include cereals and starchy roots. **95**

Subduction zone Where plates slide beneath other plates that they have collided with and are eventually consumed. **7**

Subsidy A payment to help make something profitable. Subsidies are paid to farmers in the EU to help them compete with farmers from other parts of the world. **38**

Subsistence farming Growing enough for the farmer and family, with little or nothing left over for sale. **79**

Sustainable development Improving people's standard of living, in a way that will last for the long term, without seriously damaging the environment. **40**

T

Third World An old term that was used to describe less economically developed countries. **26**

Tilt metre Measures any changes in the slope of the ground and may show when a volcano is building up and ready to erupt. **18**

Trading partners Two countries that sell goods and services to each other. **56**

Tsunami A giant wave in the ocean, created by an underwater earthquake or a landslide below the ocean's surface. **8**

U

Underemployed People who cannot find full-time work and who cannot earn a decent wage to support themselves and their families. **53**

V

Volcanism (or vulcanism) The movement of magma and gases up through the Earth's crust and on to the surface. **16**

Voluntary aid Private money from individuals and organisations, sent as either emergency or long-term aid. **21**

Index